IROQUOIS CULTURE
& COMMENTARY

PEACEMAKER'S MESSAGE

LEADING
TO
GOOD
MIND

Reconciliation
Reason
Compromise
Consensus
→ Good mind

  └→ Peace to
     naturally
     follow

A way of living
to be shared
w/ all – all
living in peace

IROQUOIS CULTURE
& COMMENTARY

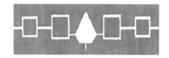

Doug George-Kanentiio

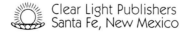

Clear Light Publishers
Santa Fe, New Mexico

Library of Congress Cataloging-in-Publication Data

George-Kanentiio, Doug
    Iroquois culture and commentary / Doug George-Kanentiio.—1st ed.
        p.   cm.
    Includes index.
    ISBN 1-57416-053-2 (paper)
    1. Iroquois Indians. I. Title.

E99.I7 G46 2000
947.004'9755—dc21   00-025867

Production and typography by Carol O'Shea
Cover artwork by Stephanie Thompson, Akwesasne Mohawk
Cover design by Carol O'Shea and Marcia Keegan

ACKNOWLEDGMENTS

I am indebted to many people for serving as mentors, friends, storytellers, compatriots, and partners in the ongoing effort to persevere as families within the circle of the Haudenosaunee. There are those who have walked on before me: ancestors of long ago, both my parents, my remarkable uncle Angus, and my grandmother Kanenratironthe, along with all those courageous spirits who dared to believe the Iroquois had an absolute right to survive as a distinct people. I also owe much to leaders such as Jake and Judy Swamp, Oren Lyons, Irv Powless, Rick Hill, Pete Jemison, Kevin Deer, Charlie Hill, Dan Longboat, John Fadden, Ray Fadden, Charlie Patton, and Eddie Gray among many others.

Central to my being are my Mohawk-Oneida-Shawnee families from Akwesasne, Kahnawake, and Oneida (numerous, stubborn, and talented) from whom I derive limitless inspiration. Tim Bunn, editor of the *Syracuse Herald Journal*, has my gratitude for giving me the chance to address his readers, likewise Paul DeMain, the valiant editor of *News From Indian Country*.

I am amazed by the extraordinary fortune that has come my way in the past decade, ever since I fulfilled a dream by marrying Joanne Shenandoah, as creative as she is beautiful. We have taken part in many fantastic adventures during our time together, much of which shall become scarce-believed tales for the next generation.

CONTENTS

I

INTRODUCTION: SURVIVAL OF THE HAUDENOSAUNEE

This is a book about the Iroquois and by an Iroquois. Its intent is to provide the reader with admittedly subjective perspectives into an aboriginal North American society.

For generations the Iroquois have served as a subject for many academic and social writers, all of whom have attempted in their own way to explain who the Iroquois are and why we are such compelling subjects. Yet there are very few books that describe our history and culture from within, by those who have had the intimate experiences that are the unique prerogative of an Iroquois person.

As a general explanation as to who we are, the Iroquois are "the People Building a Longhouse," or, in the Onondaga-Seneca dialects of the Iroquois language, the Haudenosaunee. (The word "Iroquois" is said to be of Algonkian origin; it is believed to mean "snakes," referring to the silent manner in which the Haudenosaunee struck at their enemies.)

Hundreds of years before the arrival of Cristobal Colon (aka Christopher Columbus) to America in 1492, the Iroquois had established the world's first united nations organization in the northeast woodlands, on the southern shore of Onondaga Lake in what is now central New York State. At that time (according to one estimate it was in August

of 1142), the prophet we refer to in Mohawk as Skennenrahawi, or the Peacemaker, drew together the previously
warring elements of the Iroquois into a great league based
upon the principles of peace.

Skennenrahawi persuaded the Mohawks, Oneidas, Onondagas, Cayugas, and Senecas to abandon war as a means of
resolving disputes and to adopt his teachings of reconciliation, reason, compromise, and consensus as disciplines
leading to the development of "good mind," a state of being
from which peace would naturally follow.

The united Iroquois were called the Five Nations Iroquois
Confederacy until the second decade of the eighteenth
century, when they were joined by their southern cousins, the
Tuscaroras. Together, the Six Nations would become the most
influential Native people in North America, a united league of
nations powerful enough to command the attention of
England, France, and the infant United States.

Skennenrahawi's dream for the Haudenosaunee was not
that the Confederacy would reign supreme as a political or
economic force but that his instructions might be carried
around the world so all human beings might at one time come
to know true peace. Effective communication was important
to Skennenrahawi, and throughout Iroquois history our
people have been involved in this activity on many fronts. Initially, we had a network of messengers ready to carry the news
from one end of Iroquois territory to the other over a number
of well-defined trails. Later, as we came to know the European
colonists, we implored them to deliver our words across the
great eastern sea. We even, at times, sent our own ambassadors
to Europe to carry our concerns to the various heads of state.

We enjoyed having delegates travel to our various capitals.
All the Atlantic seaboard colonies—the Dutch, French, and
English—sought alliances with the Haudenosaunee. We knew

we held the balance of power in North America, yet also realized the dangers of being drawn into the endless wars that the colonial powers seemed to enjoy fighting on our lands.

Our leaders did their best to protect our territories from unwarranted intrusions by land-hungry settlers, but to no avail. When the American Revolution erupted, the Haudenosaunee adopted a stance of official neutrality, although many of our people took a very active role in the war for which we were all subsequently punished.

Within a few years after the British surrender at Yorktown, Virginia, we were rocking on our heels from the land-grabbing schemes of cash-hungry New York. Tens of thousands of settlers grabbed as much of our territory as they could, forcing the shocked Iroquois to adjust to life on small, resource-poor reservations.

Our fall from power was stunningly fast. From being a key player in continental issues, we were discarded, ignored, and belittled. The 1790s were a particularly terrible time for the Iroquois, as the greater part of our homelands were stolen and many of our people became demoralized and fell victim to alcoholism.

Just in the nick of time, a second prophet called to us, showing the people a way to survive in a new reality. The prophet was Skaniateriio, or Handsome Lake, a Seneca chief whose health had been severely damaged by drinking. He fell into a drunken stupor and was revived at the point of death by spiritual messengers presenting him with instructions from the Creator. The Good Words of Skaniateriio were our salvation. By adhering to his teachings, we adjusted to reservation life and retained our identity as Haudenosaunee.

As Mohawks growing up at Akwesasne, my friends and I learned little about our amazing history. My home reservation straddles the international border 100 kilometers southwest of Montreal, the only Native community in North America to be so dissected.

One of seventeen brothers and sisters, I was raised on the so-called "Canadian" side of the reservation, in St. Regis Village. Our home was on the banks of the St. Lawrence River just across the street from the St. Regis Catholic Church, a Jesuit mission established in 1755.

Our formal academic instruction began in the St. Regis Village School, under the guidance of the Sisters of St. Anne with assistance from a Mohawk priest of great oratorical abilities from our sister community of Kahnawake. Our studies did touch on Iroquois history but the context left us with little appreciation for who we were as a people.

Mohawks, we were told, were biologically given to cruelty, with no more vivid example of this than the torture and execution of a number of Jesuits, allegedly by our forefathers. Burning priests seemed to be quite alien to the friendly nature of our community, but there were times, particularly during the heated lacrosse games marking the Mohawk summer, when one might catch a glimpse of the passions that caused our enemies to flee at the mere mention of our name.

A few miles south, however, the Mohawk students on the "American" side had enjoyed the benefits of instruction by Ray Fadden-Tenahetorens, the amazing teacher who revolutionized Mohawk culture by affirming the reality of our history. Without external resources, and facing considerable internal opposition, Fadden had his Mohawk boys and girls conduct primary research about their families, community, and nation. He instilled in them a sense of delight with regard to the great achievements of their ancestors, along with an abiding sense of pride in their collective heritage.

Rather than accept the standard versions of our history, the Mohawk students of the 1960s began to probe into their own past. They learned that the principal towns of the Mohawk Nation had once been located west of Albany, New York, in a region called the Mohawk Valley. When young people listened to the elders, they were told of the time when the Mohawks could call all the land south of the St. Lawrence River, north of the Delaware, west of the Hudson, and east of the West Canada Creek, their aboriginal home—all 10 million acres of it.

They were told of the decision by some Mohawks to leave that region because of European encroachment, to resettle upon ancient village sites next to the St. Lawrence, where they were followed by Catholic missionaries. The students found out Akwesasne was a former Mohawk community and was reestablished in the 1740s by Mohawk Valley refugees and their Kahnawake relatives. They were joined later by the Oneidas and Onondagas.

Then there were the stories of the Mohawk influence on the fur trade and of political discussions with colonial leaders such as Ben Franklin and George Washington on the nature of freedom. There were tales of great orators such as Hendricks, Cornplanter, and Canasatego; all of whom spoke in defense of the people.

Treaties were uncovered, wampum belts remade, buckskin clothing sewn, and the old songs dusted off. The Mohawks discovered how Native people had truly changed mankind, from the food people ate to the medicines they took. In truth, much of the good health enjoyed by the world could be traced to the intellectual achievements of the American Indian, of which the Iroquois contributions were an important part.

In time, I cast off the cultural burdens of my school and gravitated to those who had learned to stand strong because of teachers like Mr. Fadden. Stimulated by our findings, the Mohawks of Akwesasne decided to spread the word about the

Haudenosaunee. A highly effective cultural touring group called the White Roots of Peace was formed in 1966. It was composed of young Iroquois who visited hundreds of college campuses, reservations, and Native urban centers delivering lectures, holding social gatherings, and advocating an aggressive, positive approach to Indian rights.

Akwesasne Notes, a journal that reported on indigenous movements worldwide, was created in 1968. It was a revolutionary publication that sparked the creation of dozens of other Native newspapers.

Other important developments were occurring around that time. The Onondaga asserted Native sovereignty by opposing New York State jurisdiction when, in 1971, state officials attempted to expand Interstate 81 through their lands. State troopers were ordered to arrest any Iroquois who stood in the way of the construction crews. At a critical moment, the troopers were sent to Attica to contain the prison uprising there. The Onondagas also coordinated the issuing of Haudenosaunee passports, negotiated an alliance with the Lakota Nation during the Wounded Knee reoccupation in 1973, and sent delegations to the United Nations in 1977.

In the 1970s, the Mohawks elected to reform the manner in which their children were formally educated. At Kahnawake and Akwesasne, alternative schools were formed in which instruction was in the Mohawk language and followed a decidedly Iroquoian curriculum. Next came electronic communications and the formation of independent radio broadcasting facilities in the 1980s in the Mohawk communities of Kahnawake, Kanehsatake, Tyendinaga, and Akwesasne.

Travel among the Iroquois communities became the norm in the seventies as the people went from reservation to reservation to take part in spiritual, social, and political gatherings. Mohawks could be found participating in the Midwinter rituals at Onondaga or listening carefully to the recitation of the Great Law of Peace at Oshweken. The ancient ceremonies that are central to our sense of purpose and belonging in the world have enjoyed growing support. At each communal gathering, during which we express our gratitude to the Creator, hundreds of young Mohawks gather to affirm the most sacred rituals of our ancestors. Our generation can also be counted on to lend aid whenever there is a crisis, political or otherwise.

Certainly, the People of the Longhouse are experiencing great cultural and political stress, particularly in the area of unregulated economic activities. But their amazing determination to prevail at times seems nothing short of miraculous.

Over the past three decades, my appreciation for this magical thing called Haudenosaunee-Iroquois-Mohawk has intensified, largely because of patriots such as Ernie Benedict, Ray Fadden, Pete Jemison, Jake Swamp, Tom Porter, Maisie Shenandoah, Oren Lyons, Judy Swamp, and those brave ones who have passed on: Jake Thomas, Leon Shenandoah, Julius Cook, Angus George, Alec Gray, Ross David, Anne Jock, and Joseph Mitchell. These brave ones are rightly honored for their deep commitment to the survival of the Haudenosaunee.

Then there are the personal stories, which are as fascinating as any treaty council or bridge blockade. My Oneida in-laws are preserving the dream of a united Oneida nation in the face of great opposition. They are supported by my wife, Joanne Shenandoah-Tekaliwhakwa, who over the past decade has become one of the most honored Native musicians in North America by virtue of her pure talents and her determination to remain true to her Oneida heritage. It is said when she sings on stage the ancestors join her.

Each one of my siblings also has a story to tell of how they were scattered to the winds in a classic example of social services insensitivity and express cruelty, only to refuse to accept defeat. They have all outlived the system that tried to break their Native spirit, as have the citizens of the Mohawk Nation and the Haudenosaunee Confederacy.

Herein lies the amazing survival story of the unbroken People Building the Longhouse.

II

IROQUOIS ROOTS

THE BERING STRAIT THEORY

Imagine you are part of a small group of nomadic hunters, compelled for some unknown reason to leave your territory and drift to the northeast. Your group's journey may take decades to complete and might even continue long after your death. It began in the middle of a vast continent and involves moving toward a barren land of high mountain ranges marked by long, brutally cold winters.

While hunting was a challenge in your former region, it proves much more difficult as your band heads deeper into the frigid north. Finally, after seasons of deprivation and starvation, the scouts ahead of your group come to the shore of a great salt sea, the other side of which is lost in heavy fog. Ahead of you unfolds a vast plain of treacherous bog across which no large mammal can pass. Since this marshy land lies stretched between two polar oceans, it is swept by hurricane-force storms that drive the temperatures so low skin turns to ice wherever it is in contact with the air.

Superhuman effort is needed to endure the horrors of your journey, but the ever-dwindling band presses on, driven to the east by a strange compulsion that defies understanding.

Most of your group dies of hunger on the bogs, but a few manage to stumble forward until they reach a new land, void of human habitation. Once again there are unceasing mountain ranges to climb without any expectation the arctic atmosphere will end.

Finally, there is a glimmer of hope. Far ahead you spot a bright band of blue and white shimmering in the distance. Perhaps these are low-lying clouds covering a sheltering valley where you might once again shed your heavy animal pelt cloaks and bask in the warm sun.

As you get closer to the area your spirits are crushed, for directly before the company is a tremendous glacier two miles high and stretching beyond sight from the north to the south. Some of your band want to return across the bogs but others insist there is a way through the ice. As if by magic they find a chasm in the glacier. They eagerly enter and walk its entire 1,500-mile length without food of any kind while contorting their frail bodies through a narrow wind tunnel marked by 200-mile-per-hour tempests.

They emerge from the glacier to discover a fertile land of woolly mammoths, giant bison, and vast herds of horses. Your group is overjoyed by what they find and quickly populate the continent. Mysteriously, they ignore the smaller game creatures and risk their lives to exterminate the largest animals.

In time, your descendents will drift apart and within an astonishingly short period develop over 500 languages and dialects to communicate across hundreds of nations spread over two continents.

As strange as the above sounds, it is the basis upon which many otherwise intelligent scientists have determined the Western Hemisphere was first populated by human beings. Anyone with a shred of common sense will come to the conclusion that the Bering Strait migration theory is irrational. It is a theory only, for no true physical evidence exists that supports this concept. It is also illogical, for the only time a land bridge connected Asia and the Americas was during the ice age of 10,000 years ago, when human life in that region was impossible.

Then there is the other serious problem with the Bering Strait theory: it collapses when archaeologists find evidence that humans were here long before the end of the last ice age. Such evidence has been uncovered in South America, New Mexico, and California.

But if Indians did not come from Asia, where did they originate? The answer lies within Native oral histories for those willing to listen, learn, and believe.

ORIGINS OF THE IROQUOIS

Central to the beliefs of every culture is the story of where they came from and how they arrived at their current time and place. While many origin stories are almost mythical in nature, others are surprisingly consistent with hard physical or linguistic data. Oral traditions inevitably contain valuable insights into the culture and mannerisms of any people, and none more so than those people who, because they lack a method of writing, rely exclusively on collective memories passed down through the ages by the sacred act of storytelling.

Such is the case with the Iroquois, a people who until recently passed on all their history by the spoken word. How accurate are these legends? I contacted my friend Dr. Dean Snow, an archaeologist at the State University of New York at Albany who has spent many years collecting material from various Mohawk settlements in central New York.

I asked Dr. Snow specific questions as to where he thought we came from, based solely on the evidence he had collected. His conclusions largely substantiate what I had been told by the elders of the Mohawk Nation, namely that we were originally a people from the desert area of the American Southwest who had gradually moved into this region over a period of many generations.

When our people tell a story they do not refer to specific years but recall special events, exceptional people, a specific land form or unusual celestial phenomenon. Eclipses of the sun are remembered and passed on, as are political and social upheavals. All of this is brought together in the form of a story to be told by our oral historians —men and women who traveled from one Iroquois village to the next during the winter cold, carrying with them the legends of our nations.

We are told our story began with the coming to earth of the Sky Woman, a person from a world beyond the stars who was drawn to this planet by curiosity. Instead of firm land, she found endless water because a great flood had covered the earth. Only through the intervention of certain animals was she able to avoid drowning in this endless sea.

By a series of miracles, she was able to have mud dredged from the ocean floor and placed upon the back of a giant turtle. By dancing upon it, she caused this muck to grow until it became the continent of North America, which the Iroquois call Turtle Island. Heavy with child, the Sky Woman gave birth to a daughter. When this daughter grew up, she was impregnated by the western wind with male twins.

Through another series of adventures, which take many hours to tell, this new land was given form and populated with plants and animals by the grandsons of the Sky Woman, one of whom was good and the other very bad. The good twin made humans in his image but his jealous brother corrupted these early people, giving them characteristics such as greed, hatred, and anger.

In time, after a great struggle, which took place on the southern shores of Onondaga Lake, the evil twin was defeated by his brother, but his deeds could not be undone. From that day to this, life on earth has been a constant struggle between the forces of light and darkness.

Our elders tell us we first grew to become a distinct people in the Southwest, in the land where the Hopi live. Indeed, to this day the Iroquois refer to the Hopi as our cousins, relatives whom we remember even after the passing of thousands of years.

For some reason, the Iroquois began to wander away from the Southwest and eventually settled at the eastern edge of the Great Plains where the Missouri and Mississippi River, meet, near current-day St. Louis. It is said we were close allies with the Wolf Nation, now called the Pawnee. (In the movie *Dances With Wolves*, they are shown as the Indians with the Mohawk haircut attacking Lt. Dunbar's Lakota friends. It is entirely possible they borrowed their hairstyles from us, since the Iroquois were a very important political and economic force in the Midwest throughout the seventeenth and eighteenth centuries.)

After many generations, the Iroquois again moved, this time toward the northeast following the Ohio River. During the course of this journey several small bands split off to venture north, where, over time, they grew into the Tobacco, Neutral, Huron, Petun, Wenro, and Erie nations. Another group went to the southeast and became the Cherokees, while a large number settled in central Pennsylvania and were known as the Susquehannas or Conestoga Nation.

Undeterred by these divisions, the main Iroquois party continued on, paddling their canoes along the shores of the Great Lakes and down the St. Lawrence River until they were stopped at a place near Three Rivers, Quebec, by the Algonquins. It is said the Iroquois were enslaved by the Algonquins and spent many years laboring for a people we called the

Adirondacks, or "bark eaters," because they had the habit of flavoring their food with shredded bark.

After many years had passed, the Iroquois managed to escape. They retraced their steps along the St. Lawrence and into Lake Ontario. As they were about to land near the mouth of the Oswego River, they spotted the Adirondacks coming fast in an effort to recapture them. In a scene reminiscent of the "Divine Wind," or kamikaze, said to have protected the Japanese against invasion, a great storm came from the west and upset the canoes of the Adirondacks, drowning many of their men and driving the rest far into the lake.

Having landed safely, the Iroquois liked what they saw. Within a few years their population had grown so quickly that it was necessary to expand further into that territory. One group decided to set up their villages along the Mohawk River and became known as the People of the Flint because of the flint quarries in this eastern area. In the Iroquois language, they are the Kaiienkehaka, but are also called the Mohawks.

To the west of the Mohawks were the Oneidas, followed by the Onondagas, the swamp-dwelling Cayugas, and along the Genessee River, the People of the Great Hill or Senecas. Another group went far to the south to what is now North Carolina, but eventually retraced their steps to this region in the early 1700s. They are called the "shirt-wearers" or Tuscaroras.

This is a very abbreviated summary of the Iroquois story of our beginnings, of how we came to be in New York State. Nothing has ever been found that contradicts this story. In fact the physical and linguistic evidence supports what our elders have been telling us all along, namely that we are a people with roots in distant lands far to the west, but as a nation and a people we are of this land and no other.

The Great Law of Peace

The Iroquois people have lived in the North American Northeast from time immemorial; our language, culture, and lifestyles interwoven with the powerful rivers, great forests, and fertile valley bottom lands that compose our ancestral homelands.

Long ago, when the Iroquois lived as one family on the southern shore of Lake Ontario, we were given a series of moral teachings by a messenger sent to us from the spirit world. These instructions formed the basis of the many elaborate rituals that define our religious beliefs and practices. The messenger told our ancestors how to honor the Creator and give communal thanks for the many blessings of life by holding a series of gatherings inside our longhouses each lunar month. At these gatherings, one person was to recite the Thanksgiving Address, a prayer spoken on behalf of the people in which earth, water, sky, wind, insects, plants, and animals are specifically addressed with words of gratitude.

In addition, the messenger affirmed the ceremonies as a way of preserving the human-earth relationship through music and dance. These ceremonies brought much happiness to the Iroquois, but as the centuries passed the teachings became obscured as the Five Nations entered a time of fear and violence. It is said this era in Iroquois history was a terrible one during which the nations were controlled by merciless warlords and evil sorcerers, each of whom used terror to keep a firm grip upon the people. Each day brought new suffering, until the Iroquois began to doubt any goodness was left in the world.

It was then, when all hope had been abandoned, another messenger was sent by the Creator to the Iroquois. This prophet was conceived of a virgin woman among refugees who had fled the Iroquois homelands to seek sanctuary north of Lake Ontario. The messenger came in the form of a male child whose life mission was to bring peace to the world by forming a World League of Nations with the power to banish warfare as a means of resolving human disputes.

Called Skennenrahawi, or the Peacemaker, his greatest challenge was to convert the Iroquois to the ways of peace, no simple task given their notoriety for cruelty. Nonetheless, Skennenrahawi left his place of refuge, crossing Lake Ontario in a gleaming white canoe made of stone. He crossed the waters as rapidly as an arrow fired from a bow. Arriving on the far shore, he met a group of Mohawk hunters. He told them peace was coming to the Iroquois and they should go about and tell the people of the new way.

Skennenrahawi traveled throughout Iroquois territory teaching those who would listen about the rules that would bring peace. These rules, referred to as the Great Law of Peace, were to serve as the guiding regulations for all the Iroquois.

In time, Skennenrahawi met Jikonsasay, a female leader from the Neutral Nation west of the Senecas. Jikonsasay took great delight in provoking disputes from which she profited by supplying all sides with food and arms. However, she was persuaded to abandon her evil ways once she listened to Skennenrahawi explain how the Great Law would work.

In exchange for her assistance in spreading the Law, Skennenrahawi decided all Iroquois women would have a decisive role in selecting male leaders and would serve as clan leaders in their own right, as well as holding the power to participate actively in the political and spiritual lives of their respective nations.

Skennenrahawi also met Aiionwatha, a Mohawk-Onondaga man who was searching for an alternative to the chaos within Iroquois society. Aiionwatha (also referred to as Hiawatha) was articulate and courageous in his determination to bring Skennenrahawi's ideas to fruition. He met considerable resistance to his efforts. When his seven daughters were killed at Onondaga, he experienced such great despair that he wandered throughout the land, inconsolable.

It was Aiionwatha who devised the powerful condolence prayer recited before the elevation of a clan leader, words that were marked by the use of wampum, a device invented by him to record important events in Iroquois history.

The Onondaga wizard Tadodaho, a grossly deformed man whose head was capped by a nest of writhing snakes, opposed the work of Skennenrahawi, Jikonsasay, and Aiionwatha to establish a great league of peace. Tadodaho's refusal to relinquish his control of the Onondagas prevented the creation of the League. He was finally persuaded to change his mind when confronted by the other Iroquois nations at a great assembly on the southern shore of Onondaga Lake. Tadodaho was also given the position of chairman of the Haudenosaunee Confederacy, and his successors have continued to carry his name as their title of office.

The initial Grand Council of the Confederacy established a permanent format for all subsequent sessions. Fifty male leaders, called *rotiiane* (pronounced lo-di-ya-ne), sat in council as representatives of their respective nations. Every rotiiane carried a title name, which was passed on from one generation to the next.

Every one of the fifty rotiiane was chosen by the female clan leaders (clanmothers), approved by their individual clans, sanctioned by the national councils, and finally acknowledged by the Grand Council of the Confederacy.

THE FOUNDING DATE OF THE HAUDENOSAUNEE CONFEDERACY

The precise date for the founding of the Haudenosaunee Confederacy has been a matter of speculation for many years.

Historians, anthropologists, archaeologists, theologians, and amateur sleuths have placed the raising of the Great Tree of Peace anywhere from the early 1600s to the middle decades of the fifteenth century.

Most of these "experts" point to various factors that, they argue, compelled the Iroquois to join forces in the face of external threats ranging from European-borne diseases to fierce competition over the fur trade. Some have gone so far as to excavate ancient Iroquois village sites to examine physical clues that might indicate when the Iroquois abandoned their palisaded hilltop communities to build new towns closer to the natural trade routes along rivers and lakes.

Few of these professionals have taken the time to listen to the oral traditions of the Haudenosaunee, but it is these stories that might offer the best evidence as to the date when the Grand Council was first summoned by the Peacemaker and his disciples Jikonsaseh and Aiionwatha.

Like all Native people in the Americas, the Iroquois have endured academic paternalism, which discounts as quasi-fantasy our history as passed across the generations by word of mouth. Yet it is these same social scientists who aggressively seek out Native "informants" to enlighten them as to the spiritual and social practices that define Iroquois life.

These professionals grudgingly acknowledge the Haudenosaunee were the most influential indigenous people in North America, yet they dig in their heels at the thought that the Iroquois might have sparked the democratic ideals of the founders of the infant United States. They seem determined to debunk any notion that the Haudenosaunee actually created and sustained complex, sophisticated nation-states capable of exercising active jurisdiction over a territory stretching from the Hudson River to the Mississippi.

Some of the Iroquois critics will go so far as to argue that the founding of the Confederacy was heavily influenced by the Europeans, inferring that such a political system was beyond the intellectual capacity of a primitive, warlike, and stone age people. After all, how smart can a people be if they don't have gunpowder, professional armies, or the religious heritage that placed European man at the center of the universe?

Fortunately there are scientists capable of marrying hard physical data with Iroquois oral history in determining an actual day when the Great League of Peace was established. Dr. Barbara Mann, Ph.D, an American Studies instructor at the University of Toledo, and Jerry Fields, an astronomer-mathematician at the same institution, examined evidence from a number of sources, the results of which were published in the *American Indian Culture and Research Journal*, Volume 21 #2.

Since there have been 144 Tadodahos since the founding of the League, they estimated an average number of years that a person would have been in office and subtracted that from the present date. Through oral history, they also knew the League was created during the month when the corn was ripe and the grass was knee high, clearly indicating the month of August. The scholars realized that the League and the introduction of corn to the Iroquois took place at the same period, which is, according to the physical evidence, around the year 1100. Corn had been brought into Iroquois territory from the Southwest and quickly became the Iroquois' most important source of food. With corn as a staple and in great abundance, the Iroquois population increased, along with its political and economic influence throughout the Northeast.

Fields and Mann were aware there was a solar eclipse during the Confederacy's birth that took place directly above the Seneca town of Ganondagan. They calculated there were see W. Engelbrecht, *Iroquoia*, pp. 22-23 (esp. 23 for different date of corn)

eight eclipses in that region within nine hundred years, but only one that took place directly above central New York, during the time of day stated in the oral histories and in the corn-harvesting moon.

That day, according to Fields and Mann, corresponds to both physical data and Iroquois traditions. Given what the two scholars describe as "an unprecedented mass of evidence," we may safely set the ratification of the Haudenosaunee Confederacy as having taken place during the afternoon of August 31 in the year 1142.

NB

IROQUOIS SACRED PLACES IN NEW YORK

For those planning to spend vacation time in New York State, there are a number of places to consider that have special significance to the Iroquois. These sites are not known to most people and are rarely marked by plaques, yet to this day the informed Iroquois will stop for a few moments to reflect and remember.

North of Albany in the town of Colonie, where the Mohawk River meets the Hudson, is the Cohoes waterfall. The Iroquois believe this is the place where the prophet we call the Peacemaker performed one of his miracles some eight hundred years ago.

The Peacemaker was sent by the Creator to put an end to war by joining all nations in a league of peace. The Mohawks liked his plan but they had their doubts. In order to test the Peacemaker's powers, they had him climb a tall pine tree, which grew above Cohoes Falls. While he was perched near its top, they chopped it down and watched it tumble into the churning waters far below. When the Peacemaker did not immediately appear, they believed he had drowned and they sadly returned home. When they got to their village, they found the Peacemaker calmly sitting next to a fire, smoking his pipe, completely dry. It was then the Mohawks agreed to

become the first nation in what was to become the Haudenosaunee Confederacy.

All along the Mohawk River are the ancient village sites of the
Mohawk Nation. Such contemporary towns as Schoharie, Ft.
Hunter, Fonda, and Canajoharie were originally Native communities. A visit to the Jesuit shrine at Auriesville is also of interest
to learn about the Catholic experience among the Mohawks.

Just east of the city of Oneida is the hamlet of Oneida Castle,
so called because the old time Iroquois towns were surrounded
by palisades that from a distance looked like castles. The
Oneidas lived in Oneida Castle until the 1820s, when most of
them moved to Wisconsin.

South of Canastota, near the junction of Oxbow and
Alene Corners Roads, is a seldom-visited county park called
Nichols Pond. At this site the Oneidas constructed a large
town that was attacked in 1615 by Samuel De Champlain.
The park is a most pleasant corner of Madison County and
has a large sacred turtle rock upon which the Oneidas would
meet and pray.

An important place for the Onondagas is the south shore
of Onondaga Lake. Here the Peacemaker joined forces with
the chiefs, clanmothers, and faithkeepers of the Confederacy
to confront the sorcerer Tadodaho. Using the power of the
good mind, they persuaded him to join the League as its
chairman. Also important to the Onondagas is their old town
located just north of Nedrow on South Salina Street. At this
meeting place, the Onondagas greeted ambassadors and dig-
nitaries from many nations.

No visit to central New York would be complete without a
tour of St. Marie Among the Iroquois, a museum on the
eastern shores of Onondaga Lake just north of Syracuse, in
the town of Liverpool. The museum is connected with a
recreated fort, similar to the one constructed by the Jesuit

priests in the seventeenth century. Reenactors dressed in the clothing of that era provide instruction as to the lives of the mission residents, while the museum has admirable displays on Iroquois life and culture of three hundred years ago.

A drive along Cayuga Lake gives the tourist an idea why the people of the Cayuga Nation fought so valiantly to keep their land. Its gently rolling hills, sheltered valleys, and pure waters provided the Cayugas with an abundance of food, while the area that is now the Montezuma Wildlife Refuge, with its plants and herbs, served as a pharmacy for the Iroquois.

South of Canandaigua Lake, just off State Route 364, is a prominent hill that has great meaning to the Senecas. They call it simply "the Great Hill" because they believe they sprang from the earth at this magical place.

Finally, there is Ganondagan, at the junction of State Routes 41 and 3 south of Victor. Upon this site lived Jikon-sasay, the first Iroquois clanmother. It served as the capital of the Seneca Nation and currently has a nature trail, small museum, and learning center. A sixty-foot longhouse in the ancient Seneca style opened in 1997 provides Ganondagan's visitors with an opportunity to walk through the traditional domestic dwelling of the Iroquois.

There are, of course, many other sites of significance, but these few serve as an appropriate introduction to the sacred geography of the Haudenosaunee.

LEGEND OF TWO SERPENTS

There are many Iroquois stories passed down over the generations concerning the anticipated coming of the Europeans to North America and the attendant social, environmental, and political changes. When the Haudenosaunee (Iroquois) Confederacy was formed many generations before 1492, the

Peacemaker, teacher of the Great Law of Peace, gave the people predictions as to what would happen once he was gone.

He told the assembled Five Nations a story they were to tell their children across the generations. It was of events he said would come to pass. This epic would begin with the Kaiienkehaka people, called by some the Mohawks.

It was said two young men had left the territory of the Mohawk Nation on a hunting expedition far to the east where the salt water meets the land. For some unknown reason famine had struck the villages of the Mohawk people. The crops were few and poor in quality, while the deer and moose had disappeared. The many rivers that flowed through Mohawk territory were empty of fish, while the skies were strangely void of birds.

Hunger compelled the hunters to search in all directions for food to feed the people. These two men spent many days paddling down one river after another in hopes of finding game, but their luck was very bad. No animals were to be found.

Finally, they reached the ocean. Not having been in this region before, they were amazed at the many different types of wildlife in the area. But when they looked to the eastern skies toward the rising sun, they saw something glowing in the distance. Curious, they decided to paddle their canoe into the swelling sea to find out what this shimmering light might be.

They were far from shore before they reached the light, which turned out to be two small snake-like creatures, one a pulsating silver and the other a luminous gold. Fascinated by the serpents, the hunters took them from the water, placed them in their canoe, and headed back to the shore.

Believing the Mohawk people would find the serpents to be of great value, the two men abandoned their hunt and headed directly toward home. When they arrived back in the Mohawk territory, it was just as they had expected. The people were quickly enchanted by the serpents. They prepared a special cage for them on the edge of the village and would sit for hours watching the bright colors emanating from the snakes.

Soon they discovered that the serpents had great appetites. To keep them satisfied, the Mohawks had to feed them all the time. They ate everything—corn, meat, fish, grass, roots, leaves. Everyone was busy trying to find enough food for the snakes, and soon stripped the village bare of anything edible.

As they ate, the creatures grew ever larger, causing the Mohawks to build bigger cages. Finally, when there was no more food left, the serpents rose in anger, broke free from their cage, and attacked the people. The snakes ate many of them before the people managed to flee in terror into the forest.

Brave hunters decided to kill the beasts and attacked them with spears, clubs, and arrows. But the animals were by then too large and too strong. The Mohawks were beaten back and defeated.

As the serpents searched for more food, they devastated the surrounding area. Soon very few animals were left alive to feed the Mohawks. Almost all had been consumed by the serpents. Driven by their insatiable hunger, the serpents left Mohawk territory, slithering their way west.

The Mohawks discovered that wherever the serpents went they left behind polluted waters, desolate lands, and millions of destroyed trees. No Iroquois nation could stand up to the serpents. As they searched for new hunting grounds, the golden snake went south while the silver crawled north. The Iroquois could tell where they were by the loud noises they made as they tore at the land and drove everything before them.

By this time, they had grown so large they could knock down trees whenever they passed. They were powerful enough to bore through mountains and drink up entire lakes.

They had also grown to love the act of killing and would slay any living thing in their path.

After many generations had passed, the Mohawks felt safe since the serpents were said to be far to the west of Turtle Island. However, while on a hunting journey in that direction, a Mohawk man saw the golden serpent, now taller than a mountain. It was heading back to Iroquois territory.

In great fear the hunter raced back to Iroquois lands, shouting warnings as he went. As he paddled his canoe east, he learned the silver serpent was also making its way back to Mohawk territory.

What were the people to do? Faced with this crisis, they could not decide. Heated arguments confused and consumed the Mohawks. Some wanted to stand and fight, others to run and hide. Still more thought the only way to survive would be to try to feed the serpents as they had done hundreds of years before. So bitter was the debate that fighting broke out among the Mohawks causing some to be killed.

Some remembered the old stories about how the great snakes had eaten Mohawk children. Rather than have this happen once again, they tried to warn the people, but only a few listened. It was just as they feared. The serpents struck the Mohawks with hatred and fury, scattering the people and hunting them down one by one. Only those who had fled the village to a safe place near a certain mountain survived. The serpents, however, knew their hiding place and continued to attack.

It was at this time, when it appeared the Mohawks had no chance of defeating the serpents, a Mohawk boy stood forth. He said he had a strange dream, one that told him how the snakes might be destroyed.

The Mohawks followed the instructions the boy had received in his dream. A very special bow was made from a willow tree with a string woven from the hair of the clanmothers. Arrows were carved and on their tips stones made of sharp white flint were placed. When the serpents appeared, the surviving Mohawk people gathered together around the boy as he pulled back on the bow and let the arrows fly. His aim was good, his heart strong. The arrows pierced the hides of the gigantic beasts, killing them.

Mohawk elders say the story has been handed down over the generations as a warning to the Iroquois about the great suffering they would endure at the hands of the Europeans. It is believed the gold serpent is the United States of America and the silver one is Canada.

It is said another grave threat to the Haudenosaunee would come from within, when the Iroquois would be torn apart by internal divisions caused by greed, spiritual differences, and the loss of our ancestral values. There may well be, it is told, a time when the Iroquois doubt they will survive until the next day, but if the people hold true to the Great Law of Peace and follow the teachings of Handsome Lake, they will prevail.

NB 2

Threat from outside vs w/in to relations colonization

III

SACRED CIRCLES

OHENTON KARIWAHTEKWEN: THE WORDS BEFORE ALL ELSE

Native spiritual leaders have traveled the world to take part in various political, ecological, and human rights gatherings, speaking about the need to hold in check the exploitation of the planet's resources by formally recognizing the legal standing of earth's other life forms. The traditional Haudenosaunee in particular have been advocates for the eagle, tree, insect, and wolf. Iroquois Confederate law stipulates that due consideration and respect must be extended to all living things, including the earth itself. This philosophy is so deeply ingrained in Iroquois culture as to require all social, political, and spiritual gatherings to begin by acknowledging our complete dependence upon the earth, as well as our appreciation for everything that exists.

This acknowledgment is a prayer called *Ohenton Kariwahtekwen* in Mohawk, or the *Thanksgiving Address.* During the recitation of the Address, the speaker will gather the thoughts of the people and direct prayers to the Earth Mother, waters, fish life, plants, food plants, healing plants, insects, animals, trees, birds, winds, thunders, sun, moon, stars, elders, unborn children, spiritual beings, people, and, finally, the Creator. It is believed the earth listens to the words and is assured humans have not lost sight of their obligation to treat our "mother" with compassion and respect.

Far from being a mere collection of colorful phrases, the Ohenton Kariwahtekwen permeates Iroquois life and is core to the values of the Haudenosaunee. It is therefore all the more disturbing when the Iroquois themselves elect to become involved in activities that violate the essence of Ohenton Kariwahtekwen.

In every Iroquois community there are those who defy the "old ways" by aggressively converting their collective rights into controversial money-earning ventures. They will clear-cut forests, rip open the land, or destroy delicate marshes if there is money to be made; they no longer see the earth as the nurturer of life but as property to be sold or exchanged depending on the profits to be made.

In traditional Iroquois law, this act of converting collective rights results in the forfeiture of any and all rights an individual or organization, including a government, has to the land. Each Haudenosaunee nation retained jurisdiction over a specific territory, which was held in trust by the governing council for the well-being of both humans and other species. If a nation for any reason breached this obligation, the Confederacy as a unit retained the authority to assume direct control over the land until the nation returned to compliance with Iroquois law.

The key to Iroquois land tenure was custodianship. That which was given had to be returned in the same condition as when it was taken, if not better. Each generation was in a position of trusteeship for future generations, those "whose faces lie beneath the ground."

As much as there is heated debate regarding Iroquois claims to millions of acres of land in New York State, so too the Haudenosaunee are experiencing an intense internal struggle as they seek to define upon sacred ground the cosmological relationship between earth and man.

THANKSGIVING: A CONTEMPORARY
IROQUOIS PRAYER

Central to Iroquois life are the many elaborate rituals of thanksgiving our traditional people extend to the Creator. We believe the earth is a beautiful place, containing all we need to make us happy. Our heaven is here amidst the crystal waters, pure air, and fertile soils of central New York.

There have been many instances when our European guests have adopted Native foods, technologies, rituals, clothing styles, and mannerisms. It is an undisputed fact that when North Americans gather as a family during Thanksgiving, they will do so in buildings constructed with materials from our forests and in communities founded upon our original homes.

They will eat foods that our agriculturists have developed, from potatoes to corn, cranberries, turkey, and even pumpkin pie. In fact, the very act of communal thanksgiving was a specific Native custom freely borrowed by the eastern immigrants, but one we were glad to share.

On this special day, we would all do well to reflect on the good fortune that has brought our families safely together, at times over long distances, and will see them return to their homes in good health.

We are grateful to our Mother Earth for providing us with an abundance of foods. Her love for the human children is such that we have much more than we need to simply survive and because of this are moved to share freely with those who might be less fortunate.

We give thanks for those among us who are working hard to protect our Earth Mother. It is these individuals who have taken the Native teachings about protecting the rights of the unborn seriously. It is they who see beyond self and recognize there is indeed a need to consider the rights of all living species in the councils of mankind. It is they who share our love for this earth and to whom we entrust her care.

We are blessed here in North America with great material prosperity. We recognize that some among us are wealthier than others in terms of physical possessions, and that they are able to enjoy their fortunes because so many others have labored to make this so. We ask for temperance in our need for things so we might be more sensitive to the needs of others and share accordingly.

We acknowledge the freedoms that have come to mean so much to us. Included in this is the right to dissent. We as humans are gifted with the power of the intellect. Our respective societies are strengthened by the contributions of many creative minds from which we might learn and be made the wiser. We respect such differences along with the precious right to speak freely and boldly when we feel compelled to do so.

We recognize the lives that have been sacrificed over the years in defense of freedom. We thank the many veterans whose experiences are a vital part of our heritage. Most of these soldiers have come from the middle and lower economic classes of our society. When asked to do their duty, they did not avoid their responsibilities but simply asked when and how.

We are grateful during this special time for the liberal immigration policies of this land's original peoples. It was our ancestors who greeted the colonists with a heartfelt "welcome" and then gave them generous welfare benefits, including food grants and housing, so they might survive. We also provided them with education, farming assistance, and linguistic instruction so they might become what we were—Americans.

 We appreciate the principles of religious tolerance, universal suffrage, individual liberty, open government, and free elections that Native people taught to the European refugees.

No where else on earth did humans enjoy such freedom as was practiced here in America. With this right came an inherent obligation to respect the rights of all other life forms, including animals and plants. We ask the Creator for patience so that one day our African, European, and Asian residents may complete their learning circle and accept this most important teaching.

As a nation, we are fortunate in having an ongoing sense of justice. We are thankful there are those citizens who carry on the fight to insure all people on this beautiful continent are treated with dignity and respect before all public institutions.

We are most thankful for a system of government, rooted here in America, that permits the orderly changes in administration and power. We trust those in positions of leadership to act according to the needs of the people and to be farsighted in their deliberations, compassionate in their decisions, and benevolent to those in greatest need.

We give thanks to the peacemakers among us who have argued convincingly that the finite resources of this country should be directed away from making weapons of destruction and toward enhancing the lives of the people. They rightly point out that the United States should question its position as the world's number one arms dealer and use its energies to affirm democracy abroad by persuasion, patience, and the diplomatic use of its economic powers.

Finally, from our hearts we express thanks to the Creator for the children who fill our homes with the light of laughter. It is their world we momentarily dwell in, and it is for them we struggle. We ask that our decisions, both personal and social, might be made with their well-being first in mind. All children are blessings from the Creator and a sign by which the powers of the universe affirm their faith in mankind. On this day of thanksgiving may it always be so.

IROQUOIS CEREMONIAL CYCLES

Within Iroquois culture there are endless cycles of thanksgiving by which the People of the Longhouse express their collective gratitude towards the natural world. The Huadenosaunee believe the earth contains all the things necessary to live in peace and happiness so long as humans adhere to the laws of nature.

Our elaborate ceremonies are meant to remind us of our obligations to act as custodians of the earth and to respect all living things. To instruct us as to how this is to be done, the Creator has sent messengers to earth from the spirit world. These spiritual beings may take human form to walk among us, encouraging the people to preserve the ancient rituals of thanksgiving.

Accordingly, the Iroquois were given ceremonies that take place within each lunar month. They are held inside a common structure called a longhouse, a "Quaker plain" rectangular building some seventy feet in length, constructed on an east-west axis without adornments of any kind. The size of the longhouse varies from community to community, the larger ones being over one hundred feet long and forty feet wide. Inside is a single room containing benches for seating flanked by wood-burning stoves on either end of the building. Women sit in the west end of the longhouse and men in the east end.

The people are called to the longhouse when a group of individuals referred to as "faithkeepers" meet and determine when the environmental conditions are appropriate. The faithkeepers then pass their decision on to the chiefs and clanmothers, who inform their respective clans as to the day the ceremony is to take place.

Faithkeepers are selected by the people of a particular clan for their knowledge of plants and animals. They must also have a command of the activities that comprise each part of the ceremony, and must be willing to serve as teachers to pass on this information to the next generation. Faithkeepers might also act as spiritual and moral guides for the Iroquois leadership and in some instances may serve in a political capacity when a civil leader is absent or incapacitated.

The Iroquois New Year begins with the most elaborate ceremony. This Midwinter Ceremony, which I discuss in detail in the next section, is eagerly anticipated by all traditional Iroquois, since it means a chance to break the monotony of winter and to meet family and friends in a place that offers comfort, acceptance, spiritual meaning, and cultural affirmation.

Following Midwinter, the Iroquois return to their daily tasks and await the time when the sap begins to flow in the maple trees. The maple is considered the representative of all plants and is considered most sacred by Iroquois. The rising sap is the first true sign of spring, with the blood of the tree giving nourishment to the people.

The Maple Ceremony marks the rejuvenation of the earth with thunder and rain following. The Thunder Ceremony celebrates the waters from the sky, which sustain plants and cleanse the air. It is also said the Thunder places energy in the soils without which seeds could not germinate.

The Iroquois also have Sun and Moon dances to acknowledge the influences of these two entities on human society; both of these are springtime events. When the ground is ready for planting, the annual Seed Ceremony is held to bless seeds before they are placed in the earth.

The first crops of the year are strawberries, which become ripe in mid to late June. To commemorate this crop, the Strawberry Ceremony takes place, followed over the summer by celebrations for beans and corn.

When the season's crops are brought in from the fields, the four-day Harvest Ceremony is held to thank the Creator for the year's bounties. This event is the forerunner of the North American ritual of Thanksgiving. It is also the time when the hunters took to the forests to pursue game such as elk, deer, and bear, the main meat foods of the Iroquois.

There are many dances and songs ranging from personal chants to songs that give thanks for the gift of corn. During dances, such as the eagle or fish, the Iroquois imitate the movements of the animals to the beat of a water drum and the rhythm of horn rattles.

Each person who attends these sacred events is an active participant, lending his or her voice and prayer to the rituals. Non-Natives have been strictly excluded from the Iroquois ceremonials over the past generation, because it is believed their attendance would be viewed as an intrusion and prevent what the Haudenosaunee call the "gathering of the good minds."

BRINGING IN THE NEW YEAR

In the depths of winter, a small group of Iroquois meet in a frame house on the banks of the ice-choked St. Lawrence River. Around a kitchen table they gather to discuss local politics, the weather, children, and the position of stellar constellations in relation to the winter solstice.

It is the duty of this group to call together the Iroquois people for the annual Midwinter Ceremony, the elaborate set of rituals that mark the beginning of the Native new year. The men and women sitting at the kitchen table are the faithkeepers, and they are taking part in an activity that has been observed by the Iroquois for a hundred generations.

Iroquois spiritual life is determined by the phases of the moon, arc of the sun, and position of certain stars. The faithkeepers observe the heavens, watching for the time of winter when the days begin to grow in length. When they see the first new moon past the winter solstice, they know it will be only a matter of days before the constellation Pleiades is directly overhead, the final signal to begin the Midwinter Ceremony.

In the Mohawk community of Akwesasne, the Midwinter Ceremony can last anywhere from six to eight days. Held at the , the event draws people from throughout the Iroquois Confederacy. It is here infants are given their Mohawk names and adult converts to the traditions are "welcomed home."

Each day is given to a specific event, such as the naming of the children, but every day concludes with sacred dancing and a communal feast. Through the many prayers the people give thanks to the Creator for the goodness of life. Even during the coldest days of winter, when all is covered in snow and encased in ice, the Iroquois see signs of the coming spring. Their faith in the Creator does not waiver and has become a sustaining force during difficult times. Getting together with one's family and friends for a week of celebrating being alive and being Iroquois becomes an invigorating tonic during an otherwise bleak season.

As vital as the rituals are, equally important are the feelings of community, the sense that we are among a family content to be a part of a spiritual cycle that reaches far back into our history. We find great satisfaction in repeating the speeches, dances, and songs of our ancestors in ways Mohawks of centuries ago might well understand. We defy technological time to dance once again with our ancestors to the heartbeat of the earth and the music of the wind.

In our traditional society, we do not have religious institutions or priests. Our political leaders must also be our spiritual guides and demonstrate extensive knowledge with regard to our ancestral beliefs. During the course of any ceremony, they must work with the faithkeepers to insure that each ritual is done in accordance with the ancient teachings. If long-established patterns are broken, it could well bring calamity upon the people by causing confusion and doubt. Innovation has no place during Midwinter, either in thought or deed. We are part of an ancestral whole, a delicate relationship our spiritual leaders must protect in trust for the coming generations.

There have been many books and articles written about the Iroquois ceremony of Midwinter. Without exception they are analytical by definition since the writers are inevitably social scientists with a passion for details and ritual interpretation. The Iroquois find such material amusing, because the anthropologists and historians are so busy observing detail that they neglect to feel the power of Creation as it speaks through our music or guides our feet as we dance.

These grim professionals found no joy in our gatherings and made our people uncomfortable. We could not shake off the feeling we were being analyzed and placed in sterile categories. Since we were so ill at ease in their presence, our leaders decided to exclude all non-Natives from our ceremonies. We needed a place of our own, where we were free from the strains and demands of the larger world, a place where we could laugh and share without qualification.

The Midwinter Ceremony, like the dozen others we celebrate throughout the year, has grown in importance as our communities have become ever more integrated into the mainstream culture. Although our baby-boomer generation has bought into the American middle-class ideal, enough Iroquois remain true to the older ways to insure the rituals of our ancestors will continue on through the twenty-first century. That this is the case, particularly among the Mohawks, is in itself a miracle of sorts, one compelling enough to sustain our faith in the traditional way of life.

So our faithkeepers meet, watch the stars, and when it's time, gather over coffee to decide when the people shall come together and once more express their gratitude to a benevolent Creator for the beauties of Mother Earth. They will dance, sing, and feast, content in knowing they have renewed their bonds with nature and have been embraced by the heavens.

BLESSED WAMPUM

Wampum use among the Iroquois can be traced to the beginnings of the Haudenosaunee Confederacy. It is said that Aiionwatha, (also referred to as Hiawatha), was the first to use wampum. He was the principal disciple of the Peacemaker, the Huron founder of the Confederacy.

According to oral tradition, there was considerable opposition to the Peacemaker's vision of a League of World Nations unified under a constitution called the Great Law of Peace. Most of the resistance came from Tadodaho, the evil wizard who exercised dictatorial powers over the Onondaga Nation.

Aiionwatha, also an Onondaga, was selected by the Peacemaker to carry his message to his home territory. Despite considerable interest and support by many Onondagas, Aiionwatha realized he could not succeed in bringing the Onondaga Nation into the Confederacy until Tadodaho was either overthrown or persuaded to become one of the League's fifty *rotiiane* or chiefs.

Before Aiionwatha could exercise his diplomatic powers, Tadodaho struck. Aiionwatha had several daughters he loved and took great pride in. At a certain time, when the Onondagas were gathered together, Tadodaho caused eagle feathers to fall from the sky. Like all Native people the Iroquois placed a high value on eagle feathers, both for adornment and because the feathers had great spiritual value. A stampede ensued as everyone attempted to grab some feathers, and Aiionwatha's daughters were trampled to death.

Overcome by grief, Aiionwatha left Onondaga, having failed in his peace mission. He wandered southwards, stumbling to the shores of a small lake near present-day Tully, New York. As he approached the water, a large flock of geese flew into the sky carrying off its waters and leaving behind a dry lakebed.

Aiionwatha walked across the bed, and as he did so he picked up freshwater snails, or, some say, clams. Placing these on a string, he said he would wander the land until his sorrow was relieved by a person who knew words of such power as to relieve his suffering.

In time, Aiionwatha once again met the Peacemaker. The anguish of Aiionwatha was relieved when the prophet spoke powerful words of condolence to lift his disciple's grief. Those same words are recited by the Iroquois to the present day whenever a funeral takes place. As a result, Aiionwatha was able to continue his work until Tadodaho was converted and the Great Tree of Peace was raised on the southern shore of Onondaga Lake, where Syracuse, New York, is located.

Aiionwatha's string of shells was used as a way of teaching the Great Law of Peace to the Iroquois. In time, the shells used would be those of the quahog clam, a mollusk that has a creamy white interior surface with swirling shades of purple and is found along the shores of the Atlantic coast. Tubular beads were drilled from the shell and strung on looms into distinctive patterns to assist in the recitation of the Great Law and the founding of the Confederacy epic.

Quohog shells are valued because of their hardness and their purple and white coloring. Purple beads are said to remind the Iroquois of the gravity of life and their responsibilities to the coming generations. White wampum beads symbolize the good mind and its love of peace and hope. During times of warfare red beads are used to call the League together to defend the people.

Wampum is called *A-na-ko-ha* in Mohawk. When strung into belts, wampum is used to record important events such as treaty signings. It is also a badge of office for a rotiiane or clanmother. In addition, wampum has ceremonial uses. No Iroquois nation is said to have legal standing until it has its national wampum.

Much skill and patience is involved in the making of wampum. Without hard metal drill bits, it took a skilled worker many days to make only a handful of beads. When the Europeans arrived on the East Coast, they realized the importance Native people placed on wampum. Soon, European craftsmen were busy making wampum beads with iron bits much quicker than Indians could fashion by hand. Since there was a lack of minted coins in the colonies, wampum was used for a time as currency, to be exchanged for furs, weapons, tools, and other goods.

Yet wampum has always been held to be sacred by the Iroquois who first created it. Knowing this, various officials, academics, and private collectors attempted to take wampum belts and strings from the Confederacy. This effort, which was partially successful, was given the illusion of legality when New York State museums appointed themselves wampum "custodians" on the pretext of keeping the wampum belts safe. (Safe, however, they were not. Many Iroquois artifacts, including some wampum, were destroyed in 1912, when a fire swept through the New York State Museum.)

After generations of appeals by the Haudenosaunee, and over the objections of many non-Indian Iroquois "experts," some wampum belts were finally returned to the Confederacy in 1989. However, many other belts call out to us from the airless, sterile vaults of museums, government agencies, and private collections in America and Europe.

OUR RELATIVES THE THUNDERS

When the first thunderstorm arrives from the west, with its flashing bolts of lightening and shattering booms, many people retreat into their homes to hide from this terrible natural force. Thunder has the power to shatter the earth and split the sky. It causes primitive terror in the hearts of those who have yet to understand this dynamic form of raw energy.

In ancient times some cultures so feared the thunder they withdrew into the deepest recesses of a cave or the darkest corner of a building. Today, without the benefit of a convenient cave, many people retreat to a closet, basement, or bed.

Unlike Western society, with its mistrust of nature, American Indians see the thunder in a far different light. Native people are taught from the time of infancy to welcome the thunders, since we believe they are an essential part of nature. Without the spring thunder, we are told, nothing on earth could grow. Thunder, through lightning, joins with the earth to make it fertile and able to receive the seeds of plants.

The thunders also bring with them the spring rains, replenishing the waters of our streams, rivers, and lakes. Such water is necessary for life to continue, and for this reason alone the thunder should command great respect.

But our teachings go further. The elders tell us the thunder is actually a form of consciousness similar to that of human beings. We are told these sky dwellers travel upon the winds delivering the first true sign of spring. The thunders have their own society, follow specific rituals, and enjoy their responsibilities. They are very much aware of what human beings are doing on the earth beneath them and can be made angry if mankind fails to acknowledge the gifts they bring.

Along with the rain and lightning, the thunder beings carry clean winds that purify the air and lift our spirits. Has any one of us failed to respond to the "electricity" in the air just before a thunderstorm or to feel refreshed after its passing?

The thunders have undertaken another task, one not understood by European peoples, who have a bad habit of ridiculing or suppressing beliefs different from their own. We are told of a time when strange and terrible beasts roamed North America, but at a certain time were driven into deep waters and dark caves by the thunder beings. These destructive creatures are held in check by the thunders only so long as humans follow the ways of the Creator.

A prophecy handed down over the generations tells of a time when people will no longer live in harmony with nature and will forsake their ancestral teachings. When this balance between man and nature is upset, great devastation will result. The thunder beings will no longer bring their water, wind, and energy; and drought, starvation, and disease will follow. The terrible beasts the thunders guard in the western part of the continent will be unleashed to wreak havoc upon the land.

The Iroquois are careful not to provoke the thunder beings. Every spring our people hold a special ceremony to express our thanks for the renewal of life as represented by the return of the thunders. We select our most articulate speakers to carry our best words to the sky dwellers, trusting our rituals will be taken to heart by the thunders. When this is done, we know harmony has been established and we will survive for at least another year.

Far from being afraid of thunder and lightening, our children are more likely to sing and dance because the thunders tell them that spring is truly here and summer but a few weeks behind. It is a time of celebration, of rebirth and rejoicing. It is hardly time to hide beneath a bed.

ONESTE, THE SUSTAINER OF LIFE

Is there any substance more important to the Iroquois than *oneste* (corn), the sustainer of life? Referred to with deep reverence as one of the three sisters (the others are beans and squash), oneste is more than a food to the Haudenosaunee. It is the measure of the health and spiritual well-being of the people.

Iroquois children are taught that oneste was a gift to this earth by one of our celestial grandmothers who gave her life so all people may always have food. From her blood the first kernels of corn took root in the land, growing tall from her breast while the long silk of the mature plant sprouted from her hair. It is believed the gentle whispers of the grandmother may be heard when the leaves of oneste are teased by the wind, a voice the Iroquois have preserved within the sacred corn dance songs.

Oral history tells of a time when the ancestors of the Iroquois dwelt in a far-off land, somewhere in the southwest of the great Turtle Island. One day they began a migration that would take them into strange lands far across the continent.

As they journeyed they brought with them the precious seeds of a new plant that would provide for the people throughout the year. From this single plant they would make many dishes, including corn soup, corn bread, corn mush, parched corn coffee, popcorn, and corn pudding.

Moccasins were woven from its leaves, as were rugs, dolls, and ceremonial masks. Its stalks were dipped in maple sugar for the children to chew, while the silk was an important medicine. The juice made from a corn stalk and corn root was believed to aid in the healing of open wounds and skin infections. Husks were used for stuffing mattresses, as torches, or woven into baskets and shells for baking meat. Stalks were made into containers, fish lines, floats, and mock war clubs. Even the bare corn cob was employed. When dried it was set afire beneath a heavy covering so its smoke would cure thin slices of meat and fish or could be used to tan hides.

So grateful were the Iroquois for oneste, they set aside time when it was mature to gather together inside the longhouse in a grand celebration of thanksgiving to the Creator.

A typical Iroquois community would clear hundreds of acres of land prior to planting corn. The men would have the rigorous task of removing trees and stumps, a job that was particularly demanding, given the stone tools used prior to European contact.

Once the fields were ready, the women placed the seeds in the ground, usually three or four spaced about three feet apart in small mounds of dirt drawn into a hill by hoes. The mounds were fertilized with fish remains, and each seed was covered with a couple of inches of dirt.

After the seeds had sprouted, the women placed bean seeds in the hills, knowing the bean vines would support the corn as it grew. Next to the mounds they planted squashes, which not only helped the ground retain moisture but also prevented weeds from taking hold.

In a given planting season, the women would have three or four weeding "bees" when they would gather together to clean their fields of excess plants. Harvest was perhaps the best of days. The community sat together to shuck the husks and weave oneste into long braids before hanging them along the longhouse rafters to dry. Large storage pits dug deep into the ground were also used to preserve the crop throughout the winter.

Iroquois oneste came in at least thirteen varieties, with colors ranging from blue to speckled. White corn was the most common form of a plant believed by many to be the most important ever cultivated by human beings.

Maisie Shenandoah

IV

THE IROQUOIS FAMILY

WOMEN ARE THE CENTER OF IROQUOIS LIFE

Across the country and around the world special attention is given during the month of March to the status of women. In all too many societies women are denied full equality with men by custom, economics, and law, while their inherent creativity is cruelly suppressed by placing unreasonable qualifications upon their biological role as life-givers.

Fortunately, there are places on earth where this is not so. In eastern North America, nations were created with the central principle that all humans are created equal and by natural law granted an inalienable right to life, economic security, and participation in their government without qualification by age or gender.

Given the recent publication of books and articles about the enormous contributions of indigenous Americans to the world, ranging from corn to constitutions, it is most surprising to discover very little attention has been given to the unique role of women within Iroquois society. Only recently have scholars begun to examine this part of our history. What they have found to date might well serve as an inspiration to women throughout the world as they continue to struggle for true liberation.

In our society, women are the center of all things. Nature, we believe, has given women the ability to create; therefore it is only natural that women be in positions of power to protect this function. In the Iroquois world, a female baby was a blessing from the Creator because such a child meant the cycle of our generations would continue on. From earliest childhood, the girl baby was encouraged to take a leading role in her family and group, never to hesitate to express her feelings, and never to qualify her creative impulses in order to please a man.

We traced our clans through women; a child born into the world assumed the clan membership of its mother. Our young women were expected to be physically strong since they had to learn all the skills of survival in a society that placed great emphasis on the outdoor life. Before she reached puberty, an Iroquois girl would have been able to survive in any environment.

The young women received formal instruction in traditional planting techniques and would be expected to learn the many forms of food preparation and preserving. Since the Iroquois were absolutely dependent upon the crops they grew, whoever controlled this vital activity wielded great power within our communities. It was our belief that since women were the givers of life they naturally regulated the feeding of our people.

Some misguided historians and anthropologists have criticized this division of labor in our societies. Social scientists argued that the fact that the women were in the corn fields more than the men indicated that the women were enslaved. They ignore completely our perceptions of work and the political dynamics of food distribution. Simply look at the starvation in Somalia or Bosnia and see how powerful the impulse to eat can be.

In all countries, real wealth stems from the control of land and its resources. Our Iroquois philosophers knew this as well as we knew natural law. To us it made sense for women to control the land since they were far more sensitive to the rhythms of the Mother Earth.

We did not own the land but were custodians of it. Our women decided any and all issues involving territory, including where a community was to be built and how land was to be used. Realizing the dangers of wealth being concentrated in the hands of a few, we devised a system that prohibited the owning of land by any single person or group. Women controlled this important part of our lives.

In our political system, we mandated full equality. Our leaders were selected by a caucus of women before the appointments were subject to popular review. Because we believed women knew best the character of their children, it was only reasonable to have all nominations to political office come from the women.

Our traditional governments are composed of an equal number of men and women. The men are chiefs and the women clanmothers. Chosen by the people, a clanmother is normally a grandmother. Grandmothers instinctively care deeply for every grandchild, irrespective of the child's looks, talent, or intellect.

As leaders, the women closely monitor the actions of the men and retain the right to veto any law they deem inappropriate. If a male leader violates the laws of the nation, it is the right of the women to give at least three warnings before removing the person from office. Once removed, a person could never again be placed in a position of power.

Our women not only hold the reigns of political and economic power, they also have the right to determine all issues involving the taking of human life. Declarations of war had to be approved by the women, while treaties of peace were subject to their deliberations.

The Iroquois believed in capital punishment for certain crimes. Since the women gave birth to life, it was logical that they would make the final decision as to its final disposition. On the reverse side, the women also controlled immigration policies: they would decide where a refugee was to be placed within our circle of families.

Women play a central role in our ceremonial cycles as faithkeepers, insuring that rituals are observed in a manner consistent with our traditions. They act as counselors to those in trouble, as teachers to the children, and as caretakers of the elderly. They do so because we believe women are custodians of life, and the best a man can do is to protect the women as they go about preserving our nations.

So appealing was this way of life that when colonial women were exposed to Iroquois customs, they often refused to return to a "civilization" where they were considered property. A little-known part of U.S. history is the influence the Iroquois had on the development of the women's suffrage movement in the nineteenth century. It was no coincidence that Seneca Falls, near the heart of Iroquois country, was the birthplace of this long overdue revolution. It was not until 1920 that American women were given the right to vote, a power our women have enjoyed for many hundreds of years.

This natural way of life gives Iroquois women an air of supreme confidence. To this day our women speak freely and insist on being treated with utmost respect. They acknowledge no man, or man-made institution, as their superior. Women continue to be considered the voices of nature.

Although they may suffer some of the effects of carelessness and greed learned in the twentieth century, Iroquois women continue to give life and care to our people as intended by our Creator.

The Iroquois Family 57

CHILDREN ARE BLESSINGS

Is there anything more precious to our world than children? They are the carriers of our dreams and through them survive our own experiences, good and bad. In Iroquois society tradition tells us to honor our children, as they represent the future of our nations.

It is often said by Iroquois teachers that we are to conduct our affairs, both private and public, with the well being of the seventh generation in mind. This means our leadership is mandated to enact only those laws that will protect the rights of our children two hundred years into the future. It is the absolute duty of our chiefs and clanmothers to provide a social and physical environment that will enable every one of those seven generations to survive and carry on the ancient customs of their ancestors. This enormous responsibility begins with the youngest newborn and is carried on to our most venerated elders.

Iroquois customs are very specific as to how our children are to be taught. It is said all children are gifts from a benevolent Creator. When a couple learns they are to bring a new one into the world, they should rejoice because they will now experience one of life's greatest pleasures.

Many of our people maintain the traditional practices when it comes to pregnancy and childbirth. When learning she is to have a baby, the pregnant woman will seek the advice of a midwife as to diet, physical exercise, and birthing techniques. Midwives work closely with the expectant mother throughout her term, serving as counselor as well as a medical advisor. Special attention is paid to the dreams of the parents since they might hold special clues as to hidden concerns and fears.

When a child is born, he or she is lavished with attention. The entire family, including grandparents, aunts, and uncles, are involved in the raising of the child. Each one is expected to provide for the infant, making sure all of its needs are met.

When the child is weaned, he or she will spend a great deal of time with the grandparents learning the Native language and being taught the customs and history of the community. It is believed time spent with the elders gives the children a sense of tradition and belonging. It also imparts patience, tolerance, and modesty among the young, all highly valued traits in Iroquois society.

The Iroquois did not live in single-family units until relatively recently. The longhouses of old consisted of apartment-like large buildings containing many families. Everyone inside the longhouse took pleasure in contributing to the raising of children even to the point of "spoiling" them.

Unlike Europeans, the Iroquois did not beat their children. It was said that a child's suffering as the result of parental abuse caused tears in the eyes of the Creator. Also, children were never assaulted since they would then come to believe violence was an acceptable way of resolving disputes.

TO
INDUCE
SHOCK —
STARTLE
OUT OF ?
BEHAVIOR .

The closest the Iroquois came to physical punishment was the splashing of water in the face of a particularly unruly child. If the disruptive behavior continued, the parent was allowed to march the child to the banks of the nearest body of water and dunk the child's head in quickly. In extreme instances, such children were shunned until they returned to their senses.

These disciplinary actions were rare in Iroquois homes, however. European and early American visitors to Iroquois communities observed, with some disapproval, how free and independent the children acted, respectful to their elders but secure enough to speak their minds when they had a concern or opinion.

The cliche "like a bunch of wild Indians" had some basis in fact, for the Iroquois child was "wild" in the same way that a wolf or bear cub is wild. The Iroquois believed that young people must be free to experience their environment, to make and learn from their mistakes, and to grow up strong in body and spirit.

The Handsome Lake Code, the set of ethics brought to the Iroquois by the Seneca prophet in 1799, instructs the people to care for all children regardless of lineage or race. Whenever any children were ill clothed, hungry, or dirty, the Iroquois adult was to give them food, clean their faces, and mend their garments.

The Code also instructs parents to listen closely to advice from their children and to follow their words if the children speak rightly. No intoxicated adult was allowed to hold an infant since this type of touching was said to "burn the blood" of the baby. Another provision permitted childless couples to adopt a nephew or niece in order to "fulfill their duties to the Creator."

A critical element in child raising was the belief that everyone born into this world had a particular talent—a natural gift. Parents were told to watch the actions of a toddler carefully. If the child demonstrated a love for music or seemed to find great pleasure in the handling of tools, the parents were to insure the child had every opportunity to exercise his or her innate abilities. Parents committed a grave error when they tried to coerce a child into becoming something other than what the Creator intended.

As with all people throughout the world, the Iroquois often communicated values through the telling of stories with strong moral themes. A legend called the "Seven Dancers" is often told to the young people. It involves a group of children who formed their own small society, complete with ceremonies and elaborate rituals. When the parents of these seven children found out and used violence to dissuade the youths from banding together, the young people sang a powerful song that enabled them to rise from the earth and return to the stars, from where the Iroquois believe we originally descended.

The distraught parents appealed to the children to return home, promising not to strike them again. Only one child turned back, but he fell as a shooting star before striking the earth. The seven dancers are said to live on as the Pleiades cluster of stars, where they serve to remind all Iroquois parents to carry on the loving child-raising customs of their elders.

FATHERS ARE THE PROTECTORS

Within traditional Iroquois society there is a respected division between men and women. According to our beliefs, the Creator formed human beings from the mud of the earth and then gave them instructions as to how they were to live.

Women were the life givers and men the life takers, but they were to dwell upon the earth as partners. Above all else, men were to respect the life givers.

The Iroquois interpreted this to mean women would control all things that sprouted, grew, or gave birth. It was the women who tended the main Iroquois crops of corn, beans, and squash, but the men had the task of clearing the fields for planting.

Men were expected to provide whatever was necessary for the comfort and safety of the women. They had the task of building homes, providing security, and supplying certain foods for the clan.

The birth of a child into Iroquois society was a cause of great happiness. For the first years of the infant's life, he or she would be cared for by the women of the household. Births were spaced a number of years apart so the child received considerable nurturing and attention. In addition, Iroquois mothers nursed their children for as long as three to four years.

As children grew older, they were expected gradually to assume the tasks of their gender. Male children were brought into the circle of men to be given formal instruction in the skills they would need to support the clan. An elderly uncle or grandfather would provide much of the teaching, since the actual parent might be away from the home on hunting or fishing excursions. The Iroquois believed a child who was taught in this manner was more likely to master self-control and the art of patience, two qualities that are essential to the hunter.

Good health was highly valued by the Iroquois. The boys were shown which foods gave the most energy and the plants and herbs used to cure various illnesses. They were taught how to construct emergency shelters, make fires, and read the wind and water for changes in the weather. Taking the young men on actual hunts sharpened tracking skills, but before they were allowed to make their initial kill they had to master the use of the bow, spear, club, and knife.

Iroquois children learned best by imitating adults. Stories were used to pass on values and morals and were also a means of relating to the natural world. Iroquois songs and names made the children feel they were a part of nature, and animal and plant symbolism permeated every part of their lives from religious rituals to political activities.

Fathers had other duties relating to children. They were required to prepare their sons for the vision quest, a rigorous undertaking that involved taking young men to an isolated hill or mountain where they would remain for a few days without food. The vision quest, which took place just as a boy entered puberty, was a way for him to find his place in Creation. By fasting and praying without distraction it was hoped a boy would receive a vision from nature to guide him throughout his life. During his quest, a boy might be visited by an animal that would become his spiritual guide. He could also receive a personal song or chant to be used during certain times in his life in order to prepare him for the journey back to the Creator.

Once the boy came down from his vision quest, he was considered a young adult man and was expected to act appropriately. He joined other men on the hunt along with fulfilling their duties at home. An Iroquois father was able to spend considerable time with his son, since they might well be on the hunting trail for many weeks. They would need to work well together in order to provide their family with sufficient food and shelter.

Fathers did not inflict physical punishment on their children since it was a breech of Iroquois customs to strike any child. Discipline was simple but direct; the child who violated the rules that bound the family and clan together was ostracized. To an Iroquois person nothing was as important as one's place within the circle of the family, so exclusion, even brief, was usually sufficient to correct bad behavior.

The Iroquois father was affectionate with his children and free to show his emotions. He knew secure, healthy, independent offspring would stand free upon the earth, confident they were part of a great heritage that acknowledged no master but the Holder of Heavens.

MARRIAGE BINDS THE CLANS

With the coming of spring, the hearts of young people turn naturally towards romance. The renewed earth reaches out to all, whispering soft words of hope in gentle winds. Like everybody else in the world, the Iroquois were captivated and bound by love. Young men and women eagerly sought places where they could mix and mingle or perhaps steal away for a few moments to walk together along the shores of a crystal lake or amidst the embracing oaks and sighing pines.

Of course, the parents of these couples had much to say about love and marriage, both of which were subject to many customs and rules. First, any two people considering a relationship had to know from which clan they came. Members of the same clan were forbidden to marry, since they were believed to be brother and sister. The family background would come under close scrutiny to insure the prospective couple was not related by blood either. The Iroquois were very strict regarding this matter since they had an ancient fear of incest.

It was generally believed romance began during childhood. During that period the parents would watch the behavior of the children to find out which ones were most compatible. If they saw a boy and girl of different clans getting along particularly well, they would make sure to place them in each other's company as they grew older. This familiarity, based on trust, was a sure sign the couple were not only compatible but had grown accustomed to each other's habits and could speak with ease about their respective concerns.

If all went well and the couple decided to make their partnership permanent, they would seek the advice of the elders of the clan as to their responsibilities to each other and the community. If the relationship did not work out, the parents were to conduct a deliberate search for mates, a task that might well lead them to distant communities.

The traditional Iroquois perceive marriage as joining together not only of the betrothed couple but their respective families and clans. The wedding ceremony is conducted by the clan leaders, who have the couple sit together on a bench inside the longhouse, flanked on either side by their respective mothers. The groom holds an ash splint basket containing food, which represents his pledge to provide for the family. The bride also has a basket that holds clothing, indicating her promise to insure the family will have a warm home.

The clan leaders explain to the couple their duties toward each other and their children, if they are so blessed. They will ask the mothers if they approve of the union. An address to the people follows, reminding the assembly of their obligation to provide support and encouragement to the newlyweds. The couple is asked to verbalize their commitment to each other and to exchange baskets. Once this is done, the marriage is said to have taken place.

Each clan leader will then approach the couple to express good wishes, followed by the other people attending, who may do likewise. After the wedding ceremony a communal feast is held, beginning when the bride and groom serve the first food to the guests. A social dance caps the day's events.

Upon marriage, all real property is held by the bride. The husband is considered to be living in her home, on her land. In former times, when the Iroquois lived in longhouses, the couple made their home inside an apartment in a building owned by the women of the bride's clan, which was located in her clan village. She had exclusive custody of all children. If a separation was called for by the women of the clan, the husband left the home with only his immediate possessions, forfeiting all claims to house and property.

The teachings of the Seneca prophet Handsome Lake affirmed the sanctity of marriage and clan relationships. Those instructions form the basis of all contemporary traditional Iroquois marriages.

ABORTION

Abortion in Native societies is a complex issue involving family, clan, and community. Moral teachings specifically discouraged this practice, since it was believed that the Creator has assigned a specific number of children to a woman and that the aborting of a embryo interfered with this plan.

But equally important was the practice of birth control by both men and women. The Iroquois were well aware of the biological dimensions of conception. They had a number of effective contraceptive methods, including the use of certain plants that reduced the number of sperm and prevented the fertilization of the egg. Iroquois couples also were sensitive to the menstrual cycles of the female partner and knew which days they should refrain from intercourse in order to reduce the chances of the woman becoming pregnant.

Should the woman actually conceive and elect not to give birth, she had direct access to plants that terminated the pregnancy almost immediately after ingestion and without any painful side effects. This choice, while usually avoided for ethical reasons, was the woman's alone. It did not involve the machinery of government, nor did it have legal repercussions.

Iroquois traditionalists believe the rights of the unborn must be taken into consideration in the deliberations of adult humans. Every child entering into the world has an absolute right, under Iroquois law, to adequate food, clothing, and shelter. Further, each child, as a blessing from the Creator, is to be treated with respect, dignity, and love.

All the efforts of each Iroquois nation were directed at securing the survival of the children. Equally as important, and a legal imperative, was the happiness of the young. For children to be truly happy on this earth, they had to be secure in their identity, with their immediate and extended family assisting them as they grew. Nothing was to stand in the way of a child realizing its natural talents, its innate ability to contribute to the stability of the community.

Should the social or economic circumstances qualify a child's happiness, however, or if the baby was likely to be born amidst suffering, the mother might elect to prevent its entry into a hostile world.

Native people in the Americas generally believe that the present life is but one of an infinite number of realities, the essence of which is to experience the pleasure of being. It was fairly easy for Indians to trade this consciousness for another, even if that meant the cessation of physical life. Without a pathological fear of death, the Native person was not likely to encumber their lives with the accumulation of material things, instead directing their energies at enhancing their awareness through a highly developed sense of personal freedom.

For the Indian there could be no heaven or hell. Our ancestors found it most amusing to listen to the missionaries expound upon the pleasures of heaven then fight like the devil to prolong life on this earth.

It was this "childlike" attitude that so infuriated and perplexed the European colonist. Spaniards in the Caribbean were forced to import slaves from Africa because Indians would simply lie down and die if they were deprived of their liberty. Lethal poisons were readily available that enabled Native mothers to take their children with them into the spirit world as a way of preventing their enslavement.

Traditional Iroquois would then view abortion in many instances in the light of a mother's wish to save a child from a greater harm. The act itself was against their ancestral customs but necessary at times.

Perhaps instead of acting to outlaw abortion, its opponents might consider improving the overall social conditions that now discourage many potential mothers from having children.

Is it any wonder, given the polarization of American society along racial, economic, and social lines, why it might not be the best of times to walk the earth? Are there adequate resources for a healthy, well-adjusted life for all children? The planet has an abundance of resources that, if allocated equitably, could provide for the health and well-being of all children.

Adversaries might also express their "pro-life" principles by providing homes for children in need, or acting to protect the health of the unborn by recognizing their natural rights to a clean environment, a stable family life, and enlightened education—it is these things that can actually help children find true happiness in the world.

A THIRD GENDER AMONG
AMERICAN INDIANS

For many generations, Western societies have had a difficult time with the issue of proper gender roles. Christian beliefs have neatly separated the world into masculine and feminine elements but have not taken into consideration, or tolerated, variances from these polarities. From this comes the active suppression of so-called deviant behavior by homosexuals and those who support sexual liberation.

During the week of July 4, 1995, Senator Jesse Helms (Republican from North Carolina) made statements about those Americans who are suffering quite painfully from AIDS. He stated the U.S. government should stop funding AIDS-related programs because, he maintains, those infected with the virus that causes this disease have brought it upon themselves because of their immoral actions.

As a good Christian, Senator Helms believes he is being true to his reliegious teachings—which might well be the case among fundamentalists. But surely this powerful politician does not understand natural law and how it not only allows but also encourages diversity in all things, including the sexual roles of human beings.

American Indians knew this. Our societies did not condemn a person for having a combination of feminine and masculine characteristics. In fact, those who crossed standard gender lines were considered important members of the community and often held in very high esteem.

Native people accepted the general idea of creative and destructive forces at work in the universe, yet they also knew the world was not simply black and white. There are endless variations of these primary colors, which make for a more beautiful planet.

Some humans, Natives believe, are born with the ability to function as a third gender, neither male or female, but a combination of both. Anthropologists call these individuals *berdaches*, a French term referring to a young male who acted as the submissive partner in a same-sex relationship. While generally viewed as homosexual, the berdaches were not restricted to sexual roles. They functioned as partners in relationships while serving their respective communities as healers, spiritual advisors, and custodians of sacred objects and rituals.

These unique people are called *nadle* by the Dine (Navajo), *lhamana* by the Zuni, and *mihdacke* by the Mandan. Most Native nations believed they were important to the spiritual well-being of the people because they were extraordinarily close to the creative forces of nature. In a book titled *The Spirit and the Flesh* by Walter Williams (1986), the author points out the significance of berdaches in virtually all Indian communities. He notes that Native people were generally quite liberal in their attitudes towards sexual relationships among all three genders.

Dr. Williams noted that young people approaching puberty were watched closely to see if they demonstrated any inclination to live as a berdache. Since most berdaches were born as males, the elders observed those who demonstrated a preference for female pursuits. Rather than forbidding a child to act on their natural impulses, the child would be encouraged to discover what sexual role he would play in the respective community, possibly as a berdache.

Such a child's dreams were carefully analyzed. Some groups sent the young person to a place of isolation to pray for guidance from the spiritual world. The revelation resulting from this vision quest would form the basis upon which the child lived the rest of his life.

In some Native societies, a public ceremony was held to initiate the person into his/her role as a berdache. No coercion or force of any kind was brought to bear on such young people, who could, if they desired, slip into a male or female role. Certainly, the berdache had a sexual function. It was not unusual for berdaches to marry males and sustain a family. They were considered uniquely capable of caring for children, especially those with special needs.

This sexual fluidity among Indians caused great concern to Christian missionaries, who saw the berdache as a mockery of God. Using the Bible as a weapon, they acted swiftly to stamp out this part of Indian culture wherever they found it.

Although not as prevalent as in pre-Christian times, berdaches have managed to survive in many Native societies, although somewhat underground. They continue to fulfill their obligations as counselors and spiritual guides with increasing acceptance despite some social constraints. Given their traditional importance to American Indians, it might well serve others to learn from these blessed individuals.

V

Spiritual Consciousness & Traditional Knowledge

IROQUOIS NAMES

Over the past generation, the use of ancestral names by the Iroquois has begun to diminish. Most Native children born to Iroquois couples today have only an English name because it has become increasingly difficult to find elders who remember the ancestral names. As the Iroquois language begins to fade, this situation becomes ever more serious. It is believed by those Iroquois who follow the ancient, pre-Christian beliefs that children should have an identity that affirms their connection to their ancestors and to the land.

Iroquois names are handed down from one generation to the next, usually according to the individual's clan. An Iroquois clan is an extended family that has a shared identity and is associated with an animal totem. Within Iroquois society there are nine clans: Bear, Turtle, Wolf, Snipe, Heron, Hawk, Beaver, Deer, and Eel. Not all Iroquois nations have every clan; for instance, the Oneidas and Mohawks have only the bear, turtle, and wolf; while the Senecas, Cayugas, and Onondagas have all nine.

A clan in former times took care of all of its members from the time they were born until they died. Housing, food, health care, education, and employment were administered by the clans. Criminal acts and family disputes were also adjudicated by the clan elders. Clans controlled marriages and ceremonial activities, and they selected political representatives. Clan members were forbidden to marry each other regardless of their origin. For example, a Bear clan male from the Hopi Nation would be prohibited from marrying a Bear clan Mohawk, since it was believed they were of common origin.

Adoption into a clan was a matter of national policy by the Iroquois since naturalization sustained the population while giving all individuals a sense of common purpose and making it easier for immigrants and others to integrate into Iroquois society. As with the actual naming, the act of becoming a member of the traditional Iroquois took place when an adult person was brought before the people at the Strawberry Harvest or Midwinter ceremonies. In times past, the Iroquois were known to have naturalized entire communities from other nations. Once a person was accepted by a clan for adoption, he or she was considered an Iroquois citizen with full rights and privileges. It was this flexibility that enabled the Iroquois to survive through decades of disease, warfare, and social turmoil.

Each clan had for its use a certain number of names that were passed on from generation to generation. When a clan member died, the name of that person was returned to the clan to be used by a newborn. Clanmothers held all clan names in trust to be given to the children at specific communal celebrations. Individual families might also use a special name for a child, but generally the clan determined what a person was to be called throughout his or her life.

Among the Mohawks, clan names are given at three ceremonies—the Strawberry in late June, when the females are given their identity; during the Harvest Ceremony; and at the Midwinter rituals in January or early February, when both males and females are brought before the people and formally introduced by their new names. Iroquois names bestowed at any of these events are singular, in that no other member of the clan can have the same name. It was very rare for the Iroquois to be called by a name that referred to an animal. Unlike the Lakotas and Cheyennes of the Great Plains, the Iroquois did not have names such as "Two Bears" or "Little Wolf." If an Iroquois of today uses such a name, you may be fairly sure it is of recent origin and not clan affiliated.

Iroquois names reflect the movements of nature, characteristics of the land, or a specific social function. A woman might be called "Gathering Flowers" or "Bright Day," while a man would carry a name such as "Good Stream," "First Light of Day," or "Standing Corn." My own name, Kanentiio, is one handed down from the Bear clan Mohawks of Kanesatake-Oka. It means "Handsome Pine."

Having an Iroquois name is important for ceremonial reasons. Without one an individual cannot be called upon to perform any specific duty such as serving food or leading dances. Traditional Iroquois also believe an ancestral name is required before one speaks to the natural world when hunting or gathering medicinal plants. The name is important for rituals of healing. One must have an Iroquois name for the curing to take place; otherwise the forces of nature will not be able to recognize the sick or injured.

Having a sense of common purpose and historical continuity is one of the strengths of contemporary Iroquois life. So long as this relationship with the ancestors is maintained, the Iroquois as distinct peoples will survive. Names are an essential part of our cultural heritage and how we refer to ourselves is critical to our pyschological, spiritual, and emotional stability.

SACRED THINGS

An Iroquois man was walking through the Minneapolis airport recently when he saw the face of his grandfather hanging on a store wall. Upset by this vulgar and disrespectful display, he appealed to the manager of the store to remove the face. He was told such a decision had to be made by the owners, an anonymous group somewhere in corporate land. The face would not be taken down.

Such experiences are hardly unique among the Iroquois. The grandfather's image, which so disturbed the Iroquois man, can be found in museums and private art collections around the world. Carved in basswood, the grandfather image is mistakenly referred to as a "false face" mask. Its distorted features are sometimes characterized by a crooked nose and bent mouth, capped by a mane of long black hair. Its face may be painted red, black, or white, or with combinations of these colors.

The eyes of the mask are made of tin or copper with an opening for the wearer to see through. Before a mask is made, the carver must have a dream during which a spirit comes to him; it is the face of this ethereal being the carver tries to capture on the trunk of a living basswood tree. The wearer then becomes part of a society of medicine masks.

These faces are the grandfathers of the Iroquois. They are powerful healing forces sacred to the People of the Longhouse. There are many stories of how the grandfathers have cured serious illnesses, but their primary purpose is to maintain harmony between man and nature. Christian missionaries, bureaucrats, and educators have misunderstood their purpose, and many have actively sought to suppress the grandfathers. They almost succeeded.

These masks were divorced from the people by museum collectors who let it be known they were willing to pay top dollar for the faces, regardless of how they were obtained. Many members of the healing society were shocked to find out their masks were stolen from their homes and sold by relatives in desperate need of cash.

In this manner, not only the grandfathers but other sacred items such as wampum belts, eagle feathers, turtle shells, and tobacco pouches left our possession to be stored in museum vaults or hung as ethnic trophies on store walls. Many Iroquois believe the removal of these items was a deliberate attempt to undermine our culture as a prelude to extinguishing our status as separate nations.

There can be no doubt we have suffered greatly from this breach. Over the past few years, the Haudenosaunee Confederacy has vigorously sought to have our sacred items returned to our communities so they may once again be used to cure sickness and restore our people to good mental health.

A cultural repatriation group—the Haudenosaunee Standing Committee on Rules and Regulations—was formed, with representatives of all Confederate nations. Its members have visited museums in the Northeast to examine their collections and begin negotiations that may lead to the return of our sacred artifacts.

The return of human remains is also a serious concern of the Haudenosaunee, who view the robbing of our graves with alarm. No other ethnic group would tolerate the theft of the bones of their ancestors, yet Native people were expected to bear this racial insult in silence in the interests of science.

Iroquois people don't need their heads examined. Or their pelvic bones, femurs, tibias. They want their grandparents back home where they can be returned to the Mother Earth.

In response to Indian concerns, the U.S. Congress passed the Native American Graves Protection Act, which not only made it a federal crime to disturb Indian burial sites but also mandated the return of our sacred items from any institution or museum that received funding from the U.S. government. Appeals are being made to individuals who might have sacred Iroquois artifacts in their possession to contact us and arrange for them to be returned to us.

New Yorkers rightfully take pride in having a distinct, vibrant Indian culture within the state. If this presence is to be sustained into the next generation, the Iroquois must have our sacred objects back home, where they may once again be used in a manner consistent with our ancestral values.*

EL NIÑO FULFILLS IROQUOIS PROPHECY

The most recent El Niño created considerable damage in the United States as it cut a destructive path from California to New England. The name "El Niño" was given to this event by South American fishermen, who observed its coming around Christmas and referred to it as the "Christ Child."

According to scientists, El Niño occurs every two to seven years when warm water in the Pacific displaces the normally cold water emanating from the ocean depths. Accompanying El Niño is the "southern oscillation," a high-pressure system over the Pacific countered by low pressure across the Indian Ocean. The oscillation and warm ocean currents occurring at the same time result in the disruptive atmospheric conditions that bring abnormally high winter temperatures to the East while the West is repeatedly slammed by powerful storms. El Niño brings not only torrential rains along the coast but may well cause severe droughts in the Midwest and Northeast because of low snow levels and the creation of an upper-level

*For more information about repatriation, or to arrange for the return of a sacred object, readers may call Pete Jemison, the Seneca manager at the Ganondagan Historical Site (south of Rochester, New York) at 716-924-5848.

pressure system. The interior of the continent is caught high and dry between the drenched coasts.

While scientists are becoming increasingly adept at predicting the arrival of an El Niño, they can do nothing to prevent its consequences, nor have they determined its underlying causes. Perhaps the meteorologists, oceanographers, and storm chasers should have listened to the words of the late Leon Shenandoah, spiritual leader and Tadodaho of the Haudenosaunee Confederacy.

Shenandoah listened carefully to the teachings of his elders, paying particular attention to the set of warnings included in the Code of Handsome Lake. Handsome Lake, as mentioned earlier, was the Seneca leader who in 1799 experienced a series of visions brought to him by messengers from the Creator. The visions transmitted prophecies and a set of moral rules for the Iroquois to live by. Of special interest at the present time are his prophecies, particularly those that told of a time when the earth would begin cleansing itself from the ravages caused by humans.

Leon Shenandoah was keenly aware of the coming calamities. He cautioned world leaders to think carefully about the consequences of their actions when they undertook the exploitation of the living earth. He would have said the burning of the forests in Indonesia must logically result in a disturbance of the atmosphere, causing heat to be retained beneath the clouds, which in turn warmed the ocean and triggered an El Niño.

Shenandoah told world leaders the nations of the world would suffer through climatic changes that would produce terrible storms. He said they should watch the movements of the animals, particularly those who begin to disappear from the land. They have become so disturbed by human behavior, he would say, that they have returned to the Creator's land.

Shenandoah told people to watch for the dying of the sacred maples and the fading of the wild strawberries, for these would herald the coming purification. He said to take note of a seven-year span when many crops will not germinate, while certain poisonous creatures will walk upon the land.

Shenandoah knew sorcery would be openly practiced by those Iroquois opposed to the traditional leaders, and he foresaw the introduction of corrupting influences such as gambling and increased consumption of alcohol.

In the end, Shenandoah observed, the world would heal itself by fire, but those who follow the spiritual ways of the Peacemaker and Handsome Lake would prevail to begin an era of universal peace.

TRADITIONAL KNOWLEDGE:
THE KEY TO SURVIVAL

Native peoples throughout the world have found themselves in a precarious position, their survival threatened. On all fronts so-called "tribal" peoples are confronted by loss of ancestral lands, destruction of the natural environment, and the systematic undermining of indigenous values by mainstream cultures characterized by consumerism, cynicism, and indifference.

The tendency to define the earth according to materialistic and exclusively humanistic perceptions is rooted in European history, religion, and philosophy and stands in direct conflict with traditional Native Indian values. The result has been centuries of misunderstanding, distrust, and the loss of two continents by peoples overwhelmed by the ambition, desperation, and drive of refugees and entrepreneurs from across the eastern sea.

Euro-American science and technology are perhaps the most visible examples of human attempts to control the earth; now both of these disciplines have been challenged by a group of Native activists and scholars who are alarmed by the rapid rate at which the planet's resources are being consumed. Called together by the prolific Lakota writer Vine Deloria, Jr., these Native leaders have begun to examine their own heritage in an effort to find possible solutions to such universal problems as moral decay, environmental contamination, and the seemingly endless wars that have plagued the past few generations.

For too long, Native peoples in the Americas have had their technological accomplishments dismissed or denied by Western intellectuals more concerned with developing rationales for why and how Indians should be pushed aside as impediments to endless linear economic expansion. At a series of meetings held under the auspices of the American Indian Science and Engineering Society (AISES) in Boulder, Colorado, Native thinkers discussed the need to reinvent science and expand it from a physical to a spiritual dimension. Native people are saying we as human beings have entered an era of limitations. We can see the horizon is far closer than is comfortable and human creativity, however admirable, will not be able to save our children from the ecological sins of their parents.

Traditional Native knowledge, Deloria believes, holds the key to our collective survival. By objectively examining how Indians cultivated and managed their resources, we can return to a saner way of life. As one example: Iroquois agriculturalists were able to maintain the fertility of their farmlands and enhance crop yields over many years without using chemical additives. They had developed a method of combining different plants to prevent soil depletion while deterring insect infestation. For example, corn and squash extract a great deal of nitrogen from the soil, but beans balance this by replacing the nitrogen.

Not only were crops such as corn, beans, and squash grown together in abundance, using traditional planting techniques, but resource management was extended to include the planting of certain species of trees to provide heating fuel and food while serving as habitats for insects, birds, and mammals. The result, according to the journals written by European explorers visiting the Iroquois, was a region akin to paradise on earth and characterized by a park-like appearance.

Across the continent, Indian agriculturalists practiced such methods as selective burnings. During the spring and fall, certain areas would be set afire to remove undergrowth and enrich the soils. The resultant heat would also cause the seeds of certain coniferous trees to take root. Since the U.S. government and other agencies have outlawed selective burnings in many areas, the result has been the overgrowth and the proliferation of highly combustible materials, which are responsible for the most destructive fires.

Custodianship also took the form of managing wildlife. To sustain a healthy source of protein, the Iroquois hunted deer, elk, and bear, among many other animals. The Iroquois monitored and carefully controlled their numbers; no one species was permitted to proliferate to such numbers as to destroy food sources for others. Management insured healthier species and a meat source free from disease. In other regions of the Americas, Native engineers built extensive canal systems geared to specific environments, and maintained both land and water trade routes.

While this work was being done, Native health professionals had mastered such disciplines as pharmacology, psychology, surgery, and nutrition, all contributing to the development of human beings healthy in body and sound of mind. The amazing thing is that Native peoples accomplished not only all of the above but retain, after five hundred years of oppression, much of their ancestral knowledge. To reconstruct Native societies along these ancient principles and practices is the goal of Mr. Deloria and many other Native people. They believe if we are to survive as a distinct society, it will depend not on economic factors but on the preservation of environmentally correct resource extraction activities as practiced by our ancestors. The good that lies ahead, Native people such as Deloria believe, is no further than in the knowledge of those who have been before. Traditional knowledge gatherings, formal and informal, have continued to be held over the years as Native people seek to preserve the ancient teachings as one way of protecting their status as distinct peoples.

HEALTH CARE AND HEALING

In traditional Iroquois society, every individual had guaranteed health care, which began at birth and carried on until death. Within any given Iroquois community, there were a number of people actively involved in administering to the health needs of its members. There were practitioners who functioned as dietitians, psychologists, midwives, herbalists, and physicians, all working in concert to heal mind, body, and spirit.

It should come as no surprise that many Native medicines such as quinine, chamomile, and ipecac have become commonplace or that Indians developed the syringe and had a form of penicillin to cure infections, but it does to most people. They should also know that Indian foods literally reshaped human destiny by giving the world such energy-rich foods as corn, potatoes, tomatoes, beans, squash, and chocolate. These contributions to human diet led directly to longer, healthier lives. And remember, it was the Native who emphasized personal cleanliness to Europeans, who thought that bathing once a year actually prevented sickness.

In times now past, the Iroquois would treat physical malfunctions in totality rather than seeking to alleviate a specific symptom. Among Native peoples, most instances of physical illness are considered to be the result of psychological stress; therefore to heal the body, one must first determine how the sickness came about. Diseases such as influenza, typhoid, malaria, and smallpox are introduced into the body from external sources, but diabetes, high blood pressure, alcohol abuse, and mental illnesses are in many instances related to stress and are preventable and curable.

Treatment began with the patient visiting a dream interpreter or seer, a person gifted with extrasensory powers and trained to observe the nuances of human behavior. Such a person had a special innate ability to uncover the often obscure factors that resulted in sickness and would analyze dreams in the same way a contemporary psychologist does. Knowing dreams carried specific symbolic images, the interpreter would be able to address the subconscious pressures and suggest treatment.

A few such persons had the gift of either seeing or sensing the electromagnetic field that surrounds people. They would find the exact location of pain and its intensity by feeling the pulsating energy of this aura.

Other factors such as familial or social problems or dietary insufficiencies would also be considered. Acting as a kind of health resource administrator, the seer would direct the patient toward either a healing collective (a "medicine society") or an individual capable of prescribing treatment.

An important consideration for the seer was to arrange for the individual's immediate and extended family to take an active part during treatment and recovery. Native healers saw certain illnesses as a breach in the family circle. To effect recovery, they would include the immediate relatives in the healing process, for it was believed the afflicted person would recover more quickly with the participation of family.

Elaborate rituals were then performed in an attempt to draw out the sickness and restore spiritual balance. This was done through the use of music, dance, and prayer. The key was to unlock the patient's own internal healing powers.

Iroquois healing methods also included the use of purges, fasts, and steam baths to keep the body clean. If an illness was contagious and began to affect others, the entire community could be relocated while their elm bark homes were burned to the ground. This practice is not now used, but the holistic approach to curing sickness is very much a factor in Native life and in Iroquois life specifically.

There were many healing collectives organized by the Iroquois to correct physical, mental, and spiritual imbalances. These groups had rigorous standards for admission. No person, with rare exceptions, could become a health practitioner without undergoing years of training under the supervision of elders who possessed a lifetime of experience. In the old days, healers were considered born to this art, but were not seen as qualified to practice until they had been rigorously taught by experienced elders.

Since the Iroquois were collective in their thinking, they responded to illness as a group. All natural resources were held in common and given according to need. First to receive health services, food, and housing were the children, followed by the elders, then by the women, and, finally, the men. There was never any thought given to profiting from providing these services; however, the basic needs of the practitioners, such as food and housing, were provided for by the community of grateful individuals.

Every child was considered a gift from the Creator, a blessing to be raised in abundance and security. The great affection shown by these supposedly fierce people toward all children was often commented upon by early European visitors to Iroquois territory.

Some Europeans thought Iroquois indulgence of children was rather extreme because, unlike Europeans, the Iroquois never applied physical force when admonishing a child. Further alarming the Europeans was the fact that Iroquois children were taught to serve no master. They were taught to believe they were blessed with a culture equal to any other in the world and, as Iroquois, had a significant role to play in the affairs of humankind. Add to this intellectual confidence a diet rich in natural proteins and carbohydrates, clean air, pure water, and a rigorous exercise program, and the result is a society of men and women with very few ailments.

Good health, however, is not an adequate defense against all diseases. If a healthy group has not been exposed to a broad range of disease-causing agents, the immune system is less capable of resisting an alien and unfamiliar bacterial assault. This was tragically true for most Native peoples in the Americas. Unable to withstand European-bred smallpox, measles, and influenza, Indians died by the millions. In some areas the mortality rate for smallpox was 100 percent, while other groups, such as the Iroquois, suffered massive losses of up to three quarters of their pre-contact population.

One can imagine the shock and resulting social upheaval if the United States were struck by a plague that killed 200 million Americans. No area of society would be unaffected or spared trauma. Such was the case with the Iroquois, who experienced a dramatic population decline from which we have never recovered.

Most Native communities have experienced added stresses over the past few generations as the people were dispossessed from their ancestral lands, their traditional economies disrupted, religious beliefs suppressed, teaching methods discounted, and culture dismissed. Particularly harmful was the replacing of Native education methods with those of the now dominant European-based society. Native children were instructed in foreign languages such as English and French and given a Eurocentric view of the world, which was decidedly at odds with the experience of most of humanity. Virtually nothing positive was taught about Native peoples and their intellectual and spiritual accomplishments.

The end result of years of negative instruction was humiliation, poor self-esteem, and a breach between the generations within the Native family. Deprived of identity and purpose, Indians were then cast adrift to make their way in a world that had little sympathy for marginal peoples.

It was not surprising to find that many Native people have abused alcohol and drugs to mask their pain. Many of them have vivid, if at times suppressed, memories of the abuse they suffered as children when Native families internalized stress. In all too many instances, those least able to defend themselves were made victims of their parents' anger, fear, and self-loathing. Recovery from decades of pain has been slow. Many Indians have not been able to heal, with the result that Native nations suffer inordinately high rates of alcoholism, drug abuse, accidental death rates, suicides, and family violence.

Yet for some, the current situation, as bad as it is in many communities, is less a crisis than a challenge. With increasing frequency, Native people have begun to address personal and collective illness by blending together indigenous healing practices with Western recovery methods. It is a tactic that is enjoying considerable success in conferences and workshops sponsored by Native groups.

For example, the United Indian Councils of Ontario held a wellness conference called "Keeping the Circle Strong." During the three days, Native counselors, health professionals, and spiritual leaders sponsored workshops on topics ranging from "Lifting the Oppression" to "Cleansing and Healing the Hurt Within." These sessions gave native people from throughout Ontario and New York a chance to participate in classes that taught them how to deal with stress and anger in constructive ways using traditional methods. They were instructed on how to cleanse the body to make it ready to accept medicine. During the conference, one could listen to the tragic stories of lives lost to alcohol and to the testimony of a younger generation desperately seeking guidance from their elders. To clear both mind and body, many of the participants elected to enter a sweatlodge while others burned braids of sweetgrass, before taking part in group prayers to the natural world. Such gatherings reflect a desire to rediscover such fundamental Native values as family, clan, community, and nature.

While it is true many Native people are experiencing severe difficulties in their lives, some have decided to shun the label of "victim" and begun to fight the odds. They have accepted the responsibility of initiating individual and group healing by gathering together in spiritual circles such as the one in Ontario. Such methods hold much promise for Native peoples as they slowly recover from generations of suppression and abuse.

Echoes of the great Iroquois traditions, of who we were, survive to the present day. We are able to recall how our ancestors treated the ill and can perhaps begin to apply those experiences to contemporary needs. Surely we can do better than the United States, where health care has become a nasty game controlled by the political and economic elite at a tragic cost to the middle and lower social classes.

Perhaps it is time to elevate health care to a constitutional right rather than a selective privilege. For the world's wealthiest nation, nothing less should suffice.

EDUCATION

Throughout the long history of Iroquois-European relations, education has been a concern of both peoples. When the French explorer Jacques Cartier arrived in North America in 1534, he encountered a group of three hundred Iroquois at the Gaspe Peninsula in what is now eastern Quebec.

The Iroquois had traveled from their community of Stadacona (now Quebec City) to fish the rich waters of the St. Lawrence River. Cartier was anxious to find out if the river led to the western ocean and then on to the Orient. He elected to give the Iroquois a rude lesson in European culture by seizing two Iroquois men, imprisoning them upon his ship and taking them to France.

Cartier's intent was to instruct the men in the French language and then use them as interpreters and guides into the Canadian interior. When he returned the next year, he brought the young Iroquois men back with him. Instead of finding a way through the continent, however, Cartier was thwarted by the impassable Lachine rapids.

Seventy-five years later, in 1609, the Iroquois found another European guiding his ship through their territory. Henry Hudson, an Englishman, was in the employ of the Dutch and, like Cartier, was seeking a navigable way to the

Pacific. He also failed, but not before meeting the Mohawks, who expressed an eager desire to begin trade relations.

It was economics, politics, and plain curiosity that led the Iroquois to study the Europeans. The Native people quickly mastered the complexities of European affairs and for the next 150 years were able to prosper because they made it their business to understand the Western mind.

But the Iroquois realized their survival depended upon the ability to anticipate changes in the political winds while mastering the latest technologies. In 1710 the Mohawks sent three representatives to London, both to strengthen the alliance between the Confederacy and England and in response to the European fascination with Native people.

These diplomats, one of whom was a Mahican, had specific requests to make of Queen Anne. They wanted English craftsmen to settle among them and instruct the Mohawks in such skills as metallurgy and blacksmithing, while seeking the assistance of an Anglican minister to teach them about the Protestant faith. Still, the Iroquois wanted the Europeans to keep their distance. They were apprehensive about too much colonial influence in their affairs.

At the 1744 Treaty of Lancaster in Pennsylvania, the Onondaga leader Canasatego rejected an offer by the Virginian delegation to instruct Iroquois men at Williams College saying:

> Several of our young people were formerly brought up at the colleges of the northern provinces; they were instructed in all your sciences; but when they came back to us, they were bad runners, ignorant of every means of living in the woods, unable to bear either cold or hunger, knew nothing of how to build a cabin, take a deer or kill an enemy, spoke our language imperfectly; were therefore neither fit for

hunters, warriors or counsellors; they were totally good for nothing. We are, however, not the less obliged by your offer, though we decline accepting it; and to show our grateful sense of it, if the gentlemen of Virginia will send us a dozen of their sons. We shall take great care of their education, instruct them in all we know—and make Men of them.

The Seneca prophet Handsome Lake instructed the Iroquois to make use of American schools by carefully selecting a few among them to obtain European knowledge, but to insure those chosen would return to help the people. Today those lessons are applied somewhat differently at Mohawk language immersion schools at Akwesasne and Kahanawake, where students are taught to address the world in their indigenous tongue. Students are instructed in a manner that reinforces their identity, insures the survival of Iroquois culture, and honors the experiences of their ancestors.

PASSING INTO THE SPIRIT WORLD

Despite its inevitablilty, death is never an easy topic to discuss. The experience of sensual cessation is a taboo subject in many homes, so much so that when it does occur, it produces considerable trauma.

Iroquois philosophers would say a healthy approach to living requires an emotional acceptance of death as an integral part of all cultures, regardless of how it is perceived. Denial of its central significance to us all is a vain attempt to frustrate natural law; such a breach can only prolong our grief while compromising the responsibilities of the living.

During the past decades, considerable speculation and empirical research has been devoted to the act of dying.

Certain phenomena, apparently universal, have been observed by individuals declared clinically dead who have been later revived. Those who have passed into the spirit world are said to have found the experience rather pleasant. They enjoyed a feeling of being bathed in gentle warmth while being pulled toward a bright, hypnotic light. Their spirits rose from the shell of their bodies up in a specific direction. Waiting for them were deceased family members and friends, all of whom welcomed them to the next dimension. Those who returned were given the choice of either remaining among the spirits or remaining in the physical world. Some Iroquois who went through this experience reported that they were actually pushed back and told to go back to the earth state, because certain obligations were not yet completed.

Unlike Christians, the Iroquois have always devoted considerable thought and a great part of their ritual lives toward understanding death. Traditional Iroquois believe every person has a set number of days upon this earth, and while here they are to make effective and good use of their senses.

We are all "divine" in one way: our spirits are not of this earth but are directed here from another realm. This is a place of learning, a place where we are to take delight in its beauties while enhancing our human sensitivities.

As custodians of earth, we are required to keep it in a pure state, not only for the use of the coming generations but for all species of life. By demonstrating compassion, we sharpen our senses and increase our awareness. Intellectual knowing is a logical extension of our innate intelligence, but of greater importance is our latent ability to be cognizant of ourselves within the interlocking cycles of life.

Nothing in nature truly ends; the cessation of life in one organism means sustenance for another and the subsequent transformation into something else. The Iroquois believe we as humans have been given this form of life so we may become sensual beings, to understand birth, struggle, love, and death.

Life is indeed a gift from the universe. Since it is both precious and fleeting, we have, according to Iroquois custom, an obligation to live in harmony with the earth. We can do so by following the rhythms of the natural world through the observance of rituals that remind us of our place and specific responsibilities.

A philosophy that considered the world profane was alien to the Iroquois. How could we deny the significance of what we could see around us? Was it logical to dismiss the love of the broad rivers, great forests, bountiful animal life, and rich soils of our ancestral lands as the "worship of false gods"?

Alien, too, was a religion proclaiming, as Catholics and many Protestants do, that children are born stained by the sin of Adam and Eve. We see children as a great blessing from a Creator who has given us the opportunity to become involved in the affirmation of life. A concept such as original sin is but one way of shackling the human spirit and instilling in people a deep sense of guilt and shame, emotions that have no place in a child's reality. Some Protestants believe this world is an obstacle to be overcome, one full of temptations. By remaining detached from the earth or by viewing the planet as but a vehicle for man's use, temptation can be overcome in the expectation of celestial rewards.

Iroquois who have had a near-death experience recall it as a form of knowing. They tell of rising to an all-encompassing light toward a place without pain where they are greeted by beloved relatives and friends. It is from this place the soul is guided toward a celestial home.

In Iroquois cosmology there is no "heaven" or "hell," nor is there a singular, all-powerful supreme being waiting to exercise divine wrath against those who have violated sectarian law. There are two forces we acknowledge as "creators," one with the power to bring beauty and goodness to the earth and the other, a life-taker and carrier of evil. In Iroquois society the challenge is to achieve goodness by living in a condition of material simplicity while performing acts of kindness. The resulting peace is called the "good mind," which, when achieved, makes the transition to the spirit world a simple one.

True Iroquois do not fight this world, they do not battle with death, nor do they deny its rightful place. They do not have the notion of "hell" in the biblical sense. Spiritual damnation occurs when a spirit's journey is denied in one way or another and is caught between realities—then the person is refused the healing light and cannot reach the healing love of the family.

Those who violate the good Creator's instruction by committing acts of evil will suffer by having their souls confined between the spiritual and physical worlds: they are prevented by their own deeds from returning to the Creator, but at the same time are helpless witnesses to the living. It is said there is no greater agony.

Two reasons for the current social troubles in America, the Iroquois believe, are its legacy of interfering with the dead and Western society's refusal to openly acknowledge what is both natural and reasonable. We must accommodate the dead and our own mortality. But in America, the opposite is happening. Take a stroll through any supermarket, drugstore, or mall. Literally billions of dollars are being spent on the futile attempt to prolong youth and thereby hold off death. It is one thing to improve one's appearance through the use of cosmetics and quite another to create a culture that places an unhealthy emphasis on staying forever young.

Old-time Iroquois appreciated youth as much as any other people, but they also took pleasure in growing old because it was for them a time when they were held in very high esteem. By no means did the Iroquois look forward to dying, because they believed life was a great gift to be cherished in all of its infinite forms. In addition, traditional Iroquois were taught that all people have important obligations to the living, which could not be casually disregarded. The older years were also a time for them to pass on their life experiences before dying, an experience they called "going home."

The Iroquois knew there was another world beyond this. They referred to the act of leaving this reality as taking a journey among the stars, when a spirit experienced the exhilaration of being released to the universe. If the preparations for this passage were correctly made on this earth, the spirit was said to be ready to see the face of the Creator and experience an unrestrained freedom to flow across the dimensions.

The death of a family member or someone we truly care about is the most tragic of human experiences, yet the ancient teachings of the Iroquois give the bereaved assurances that spiritual consciousness does not end with the demise of the body. As Iroquois we are taught that our souls are not of this earth, but originated in another dimension to which we return when our time on this land is completed.

As the last breath is expelled by the dying, the soul rises above the body, where it experiences a sense of peace. The soul is aware of the circumstances of death, and the initial feelings of trepidation are replaced with a profound sense of release. It is said the movement into physical death takes the soul into warm, living light where we are met by our spiritual guardians and taken along a journey into the sky. We are told this "walk among the stars" follows the path of the Milky Way galaxy.

In traditional families there is a mourning period— usually ten days—that begins when the loved one passes on. The entire clan of the deceased goes into mourning, and the other clans assume responsibility for the funeral. They will cleanse the body, organize the services, and prepare the grave. Services are usually held in the communal longhouse, with each person sitting according to their respective clan. A speaker, perhaps a chief or faithkeeper, is selected to deliver the words of condolence to the relatives of the deceased. These words were carefully chosen many generations ago and are meant to relieve sorrow by assuring the mourners their loved one is beyond suffering and in a place where their ancestors are embracing them.

It is important to know how to release an earth-bound spirit. Traditional Iroquois believed great harm could be done to a family or community if the spirits of the dead were not properly released from the earth; hence elaborate ceremonies were practiced by the Iroquois to effect planetary separation. In the same spirit, the Iroquois did not construct monuments to the deceased. Instead, they insured that anything that could hold the spirits hostage, such as their possessions, were distributed throughout the community.

After the mourning period, a family was expected to return to their normal duties. It was, after all, the obligation of the living to do just that: live.

The Iroquois would affirm that there is an "afterlife" and those whom we loved are waiting for us on the other side. They would agree that when one dies, there is the experience of being released to a pulsating light. They would say that our spirits are part of a divine whole, imparted to us as individuals but for a short while, that we might experience this planet before moving on to the next reality and finally, back to the center, to the totality of all things, the conscious Creator.

All are encouraged to dwell in peace, knowing that when their own life's journey is complete, there will be a welcome for them in the spirit world.

VI

NATURE'S LAW

TRADITIONAL LEADERS

Many generations before the arrival of Europeans in North America, a prophet journeyed among the hostile Iroquois carrying with him the powerful belief that these most terrifying of peoples could become advocates for natural law and universal peace. This prophet was called by the Iroquois the Peacemaker (in Mohawk: Skennenrahawi). On the southern shores of Onondaga Lake, in what is now central New York state, he led the formation of a union of nations conceived in democracy and guided by the principles of constitutional government as embodied in the Great Law of Peace.

Where warlords and dictators held sway, he placed in positions of authority true servants of the people, leaders void of personal ambitions other than to work in the best interest of their nations. The Peacemaker set firm rules for the selection of traditional Iroquois chiefs, emphasizing the need for each male and female leader to act as both spiritual and civil counselors to the people. He believed no one could be entrusted with power who did not have a firm command of the elaborate religious rituals that define Iroquois beliefs and maintain harmony between humanity and nature.

He created a four-tiered leadership nomination and review process, which is designed to prevent the rise of any single ruler. Any potential Iroquois representative is first selected by the female spokesperson from the large families called clans. This clanmother has to guarantee that the candidate is free from such motives as greed, a lust for power, envy, and malice. In addition, the potential leader must see beyond his time and be willing to enact only laws and policies that protect the sovereign rights of the people for seven generations to come.

Iroquois council members have to have a stable family life, demonstrate great patience, and be willing to accept the inevitable criticisms of their community. Called rotiiane, literally "good people," they are required to live a life of material simplicity since the traditional Iroquois believed the single-minded pursuit of wealth inevitably led to corruption.

Once chosen by the clanmother, the candidate is brought before an open assembly of the clan, which can either approve or reject the candidate, with every clan member having the right to express his or her opinion freely. Once clan consensus is reached, the nomination is sent to the respective Iroquois nation's council of chiefs for approval or denial. If the candidate is not endorsed by the national government, the clan has to withdraw the nominee and renew the search.

To install one of the fifty titled leaders of the Iroquois Confederacy, a meeting of all rotiiane, called the Grand Council, will be assembled. If approved, the candidate becomes a rotiiane and holds his position for life or until illness prevents him from carrying out his duties. The rotiiane may also be removed from office for corruption, adopting another religious faith, encouraging violence, lying, shedding blood, committing immoral acts, or breaching the Great Law of Peace. It is the rotiiane's clanmother who is empowered to remove him from office.

Such was the leadership selection system put into place by the Peacemaker long ago. It is designed to protect the rights of the Iroquois people and to preserve their way of life throughout the ages. It survives to the present day, a testament to the enduring quality of the world's oldest democracy.

CRIME AND PUNISHMENT

Hundreds of years ago, before the coming of our prophet the Peacemaker, human life was held in little regard by the Iroquois. Existence could be stamped out at the mere whim of one of the many dictators and warlords who then ruled Iroquois society.

While manslaughter, rape, and assault were considered serious enough to warrant execution, these were seen as crimes against the individual and in most cases the result of momentary rage and the loss of self control. Punishment was determined by a community's ruler; if the decision was for death, the condemned was brought before a public assembly and quickly dispatched by a blow to the back of the head by a heavy wooden club.

A far more serious problem for the regional despot were those who organized against the state or were independent of mind and action. For these few the most severe penalties were imposed, including the liberal use of torture. Fire was the most common method used to inflict severe pain; burning coals and red hot sticks were applied to fingers, legs, eyes, and abdomen.

It was important for the dictator to involve every community member in the act of torture, for by doing so this act of horror was shared collectively. The pain of the victim became a deeply personal experience for everyone and served to deter acts of dissent or rebellion.

Fire as punishment for antisocial behavior was by no means a distinctly Iroquois characteristic. In Europe, mass executions were common as late as the seventeenth century as the Catholic Church attempted to quell dissent by holding public burnings. Notorious inquisitions were held under the authority of the Church. The accused appeared without legal counsel or the right to review evidence, confront witnesses, or appeal an Inquisitor's verdict. Like the Iroquois, the Church used the agony of the prisoner to provide a terribly oppressed people with a temporary release of emotions, while confirming the ubiquitous powers of an institution that was, and is, completely autocratic.

Until very recently such rights as freedom of expression, worship, and assembly and the idea of popular government were alien to most people, while institutions that exploited the mind and body were painfully familiar. This was true in Europe and in many parts of the pre-Columbian Americas.

Terror knows no political bounds, as the ancient Iroquois knew. They made fear an integral part of state policy. The Iroquois would take pleasure in capturing an opponent during one of their frequent wars, because the prisoner would provide them with days of perverted entertainment. But not only that: if a man displayed particular courage under pain, the Iroquois would "honor" such stoicism by eating that person's heart.

Such acts earned the Iroquois a reputation throughout the Northeast for unparalleled cruelty. As one example, the name "Mohawk" is said to mean "man eater" in the language of the Algonquins, a northern people whom the Iroquois were believed to have found particularly tasty.

Yet as horrible as the Iroquois were, the faith of one man initiated a profound change in their history. The Peacemaker labored for years to persuade the Iroquois that by adopting his democratic principles they could secure a better life. He took particular aim at the idea of state-sanctioned acts of revenge. A primary cause of the tensions that had caused the Iroquois to split into innumerable factions was "eye-for-an-eye" retaliation when a person, family, or community felt it had been harmed. So intertwined were Iroquois families that an injury to one was taken as an affront to the individual's entire clan. Blood feuds of many years' duration consumed the physical resources of the people while preventing unification in such critical areas as defense, food production, resource management, justice, and government.

The Peacemaker reasoned that since all dictators rule through fear and profit by creating artificial social divisions; by eliminating the root cause of terror and vengeance, true healing could begin and reason could be restored to the minds of the cruel Iroquois. Where reason flourished, he thought, no dictator could remain in power. If such a simple miracle as justice rooted in compassion could change a people fascinated by violence, might his powerful ideas also alter the destiny of humanity as a whole?

Compelled to come up with a solution to the problem of bloody revenge, the Peacemaker decided that compensation of the victim's family would provide a reasonable alternative. If a person was killed by an act of violence, it was seen as a matter for the family and clans to decide. A capital crime such as murder was an act punishable by death, banishment, compensation, or adoption.

A hearing was held before a gathering of the clan leaders, and the crime was discussed. The accused was given an opportunity to raise a defense, but if the evidence proved to be sufficient for conviction, the actual punishment was given over to the family who had suffered the loss.

They were given strict options, however. Execution was one, but it was considered more important to restore balance among the clans. This could be done by having the guilty person provide permanent compensation for the bereaved family according to the particular function of the victim. For instance, if the dead person had been a farmer and the primary means of support for his or her family, the convicted person would be required to assume those obligations as long as necessary.

A similar option involved service, loss of identity, and adoption. Since all acts of violence against a person were also an assault upon the clan, whoever wrongfully took a life could be bound over to the clan to serve the needs of that clan for as long as they deemed proper. After good faith and genuine remorse had been demonstrated, the clan had the option of adopting the offender to replace the victim. If this was done, the convicted person completely lost his or her former identity, including name, clan affiliation, and previous national and work status.

A fourth type of punishment was to physically scar the guilty party and banish him from the community. By selecting this option, further bloodshed was avoided and the criminal became an "untouchable" wherever he went, forever shunned by all Native nations. It was said this fate almost inevitably resulted in quick spiritual and physical death, since the Iroquois valued family above all else and to be excluded was to remove a person's most intimate sense of self. Without this inner substance, the outer shell would rapidly wither and die.

In instances of rape, an unusual occurrence in Iroquois society, the perpetrator was branded with a certain mark on the face and driven from his community. The Iroquois believed few crimes were as repulsive as those against women.

In all instances, the intent was to effect healing and break the cycle of violence, either by individuals or the state. The founding of the Haudenosaunee (Six Nations Iroquois) Confederacy is a testament to the Peacemaker's success in breaking this cycle. The Confederacy is the world's oldest democratic government, which has as its heart the securing of universal peace by redefining and constraining organized and impulsive acts of revenge.

Our Peacemaker had a true aversion to conflict and violence. He believed the human spirit had divine origins, but the intellect of men was qualified by brutal physical passions. If guided by reason and a sense of justice, human beings could then metamorphose into the high spiritual beings they were destined to be. Without this fundamental change in consciousness, the Peacemaker knew, humans would remain shackled by greed, hatred, and fear and so possessed by selfishness as to remain blind, insensate, and deaf to the infinite wonders of a benevolent creation.

HOW THE IROQUOIS DEALT WITH WIFE BEATERS

One of the positive things to come out of the O.J. Simpson case is an increased awareness of wife abuse, a problem that has been determined to be more widespread than the public might have believed. Such tragedies are not limited to American society at large, but also occur within Native communities where, until recently, the act of striking a woman was shocking because of its rarity.

There are many causes for this change in attitude toward Native woman, much of it learned from the media, but most incidents of spousal violence stem from the radical social, economic, physical, and psychological changes experienced by Native people. Having been dissuaded by the Christian church, unsympathetic educational institutions, and a hostile state from preserving the ancestral values, some Indian males have imitated the exploitative and violent habits of their non-Native counterparts and have begun to beat their wives as a means of expressing negative emotions.

Such hostility toward women has become deeply ingrained in European-based societies, in which females were, until our grandmother's time, treated by law and custom as mere appendages of the husband, father, or eldest brother. Without the right to vote and dissuaded from holding public office, women in the United States were considered mere chattel or property, to be used in many instances to further the social designs of the male head of household.

Incredible as it now seems in retrospect, women in America had virtually no access to political power and therefore were effectively prevented from initiating the radical changes necessary to make spousal abuse the crime it truly is. This situation has begun to change only recently and the media have finally begun using their enormous powers to carry stories about this serious problem.

In the past, such an issue was nonexistent in Iroquois society. Women were the heart of the Iroquois nation and as such commanded great respect. They played central roles in the social, familial, economic, and political lives of the Iroquois. In all respects they were on a par with the males and in some instances actually wielded greater authority.

Certainly in the area of domestic relations the women served as arbitrators in family disputes, with the eldest female in a given family or clan having the power to adjudicate violations of the ancient laws. Since young couples dwelled in a longhouse along with several other families and worked cooperatively to care for the children and secure food, a great deal of stress experienced by today's families did not exist. All the resources of a particular clan or village were shared equally, including medical care, child rearing, and support for the elders.

When a couple were married, they went to live in a longhouse owned by the women in the home community of the bride. In the Iroquois way, all real property came under the control of the women, as did most economic activities. Children were born into the mother's clan and throughout their lives sought comfort and advice from the clanmothers, the female leaders. It was the women who nominated and deposed all leaders, while they also played central roles in the religious practices of the Iroquois. Such respect for women was, the Iroquois believed, a simple recognition of natural law as determined by the Creator.

As far as can be determined, no where else on earth were women held in such high esteem or had such great influence as among the Iroquois. One can well imagine the shock the Europeans felt when they first observed the Iroquoian model of democracy at work.

But the Iroquois could be very human in their shortcomings. There were times when men would violate the traditional customs by striking a woman. When this happened, the response by the clan was immediate and direct.

An investigation would be conducted as to the reasons for the abuse. If the family was without adequate food and shelter, the community would assume some responsibility. All other possible factors would be examined. In the end, the leaders of the clan might decide the couple were simply incompatible and order the dissolution of the marriage. If this occurred, the husband was expelled from the home and the community, carrying away nothing but his clothing and tools. Thereafter, the husband had no rights except those the offended clan might elect to give him.

In extremely rare instances, the clan might permit him to stay. If he committed another act of violence against his wife, the clan would then act in a more radical way. The women of the clan would line up in two parallel rows facing each other. Each one would be carrying a stick or club. The offending husband would be escorted by the men to one end of the line and told to run as fast as he could through the two rows of women.

As he ran, the women would strike him as often and as hard as they could until he either made it to the end of the line or was beaten senseless. In either instance, the bleeding offender was thrown out of the village, never to return. The scars on his face, arms, and back would tell everyone he was a wife beater and not to be trusted with another marriage.

Such methods were highly effective in preventing wife abuse, but they were resorted to only rarely because respect for the "life givers" was instilled in all Iroquois from the time of birth. We have changed considerably since then, and many would say it might well be time to revive the practice our European observers called the gauntlet.

Many Americans might recoil at the thought of administering such a beating; this act would, however, compare minutely to the shame, pain, and terror of a wife bludgeoned by an enraged husband.

IROQUOIS JUSTICE

Historically the accepted view regarding aboriginal justice is that Native peoples were less concerned with dispassionate efforts to resolve human disputes than with exacting swift and brutal revenge for any slight, perceived or real. If one were to rely exclusively on the written record, no other conclusion is possible. Jesuits, Protestant missionaries, government agents, and explorers wrote lurid, often fantastic, prose to describe how Native people extracted great pain from any individual found guilty of violating Indian law.

Torture was both casual and commonplace. It was applied with vigor especially to those Europeans who were advocates of Christianity. Crimes of attachment or assault were punished with one swift swing of a heavy war club delivered to the skull of the victim while the tribe went into a frenzy of blood lust.

This is the damaging stereotype that has long served the oppressive designs of various political, economic, and sectarian groups to the dismay of the Native people. These damning images contributed significantly to the destruction of aboriginal self-esteem, which in turn led directly to substance abuse and the myriad of social problems now experienced within all Native communities.

Only recently have scholars, Native rights leaders, and experts on traditional aboriginal customs begun to challenge these racial myths. From this recent work, Native people can begin to extract the truth and to apply the legal and judicial practices of their traditional heritage to current circumstances. The attempt to revive the ancestral laws has now become for some an appealing alternative to depending on the Napoleonic Code and the laws of Anglo-North American society. Given the disproportionate numbers of Indians in prisons throughout this continent, it is clear a different approach to justice on Native lands is urgently needed.

Traditional Iroquois law exists in three forms. The Great Law of Peace is the constitution for all Iroquois. The Great Law defines the powers of each nation and guarantees certain freedoms for the people. It is supported by the Handsome Lake Code, a set of rules that define communal relationships and provide standards for ethical behavior. Finally, there is customary, or common law, which is not codified but handed down across the generations.

Iroquois law exists in opposition with the judicial and administrative claims over Native territory by Canada and the United States. The Americans maintain Congress has the ultimate authority over Native people, a position sustained by the U.S. Supreme Court. In 1948 and in 1952,

Congress enacted legislation that gave New York State criminal and civil jurisdiction on all Iroquois land within its boundaries. The Haudenosaunee have vigorously opposed these laws.

Also of serious concern to the traditional Iroquois is the acceptance of New York authority by the so-called "elective" tribal councils at Cattaraugus-Allegany and Akwesasne. On these reservations, tribal officials use their Native police to enforce state laws. On Oneida Territory, the leadership has secured a "deputization" agreement with Madison and Oneida counties that gives tribal police officers the power to make arrests using state law.

There are Native police agencies at Cattaraugus, Allegany, Oneida, Kahanawake, Kanehsatake, Oshweken, Akwesasne, and Tyendinaga. The Iroquois communities on the "Canadian" side are empowered to enforce provincial and communal statutes. Each Iroquois reserve in Canada has drafted its own set of local laws, which are either approved or rejected by the federal government in Ottawa. Agreements are made with the provinces for the imprisonment of individuals found guilty of serious crimes on the reserves.

There are no prisons on any Iroquois territory. All of the hundreds of Iroquois in U.S. prisons are there for violating U.S. federal and New York State laws. Their imprisonment is a clear breach of the 1794 Treaty of Canandaigua that the Haudenosaunee have been attempting to rectify. Most are in prison for acts of violence or theft committed while the person was intoxicated or under the influence of narcotics. Under traditional Iroquois law, there is no provision for a prison system; instead, those found in violation of communal standards are punished through community service and may be compelled to provide compensation for acts such as theft and destruction of property.

The Mohawk terrritory of Akwesasne, which is divided in half by the U.S.-Canadian border, has long been a jurisdictional nightmare for Canadian and American authorities. In 1892, New York State created the St. Regis Tribal Council and gave it jurisdiction south of the border, while on the Canadian side, the St. Regis Band Council (now the Mohawk Council of Akwesasne) held very limited sway. A significant percentage of the Mohawk people, however, supported the ancestral Mohawk Nation Council of Chiefs, which refused to recognize the border and to this day claims it is the singular, indigenous government of all Mohawks.

Further complicating life for the Mohawks are the territorial and legal claims of Quebec, Ontario, and New York State, since parts of Akwesasne are in each jurisdiction. In addition, four U.S. police agencies, along with the Canadian RCMP, OPP, Canada Customs, and the intensely disliked Sûreté du Quebec, bring various procedures to bear on Akwesasne's residents, and all enforce different non-Mohawk laws. Left bewildered are the constables of the Mohawk Police Force, who must somehow try to keep the peace while restricted to Canada. Attempts to apply this tangle of alien rules has resulted in legal paralysis at Akwesasne, a type of jurisdictional shock that leaves no single official, judge, social worker, teacher, or police officer able to work effectively.

Credit the good people of Akwesasne with trying to come up with solutions to this crisis. In the late 1980s, they reached back into their history to create a unique justice system based on traditional laws and customs, which, if given the chance, might well be flexible enough to deal with contemporary issues.

Called the "Code of Offenses and Procedures of Justice for the Mohawk Nation of Akwesasne," this proposed set of rules would apply one legal standard for every person, Native or not, at Akwesasne. Efforts to put the code into effect were defeated.

To understand how Iroquois traditional justice can be adapted to deal with contemporary conditions, it is useful to look at the features of Akwesasne's proposed code. The code de-emphasizes crimes against property and stresses the need for reconciliation, mediation, compromise, and consensus, as well as the need to protect Indian rights for the coming generation. Included in the code are standards for communal behavior, protection of wildlife, and strict regulations to prevent contamination of the earth. It also defines the crimes of murder, assault, and smuggling and includes statutes regulating vehicles and provisions against the sale and abuse of harmful substances.

The code would be applied by "Justice Chiefs" who would meet strict requirements, not the least of which is compassion. For the most part, jail time would be replaced with community service and restitution. There would be no need for lawyers or trial by jury, since cases would be settled by arbitration rather than by the confrontational Western system. It also emphasizes that the rights of the collective are more important than those of the individual. This feature caused many Western-trained lawyers to look at the code with alarm.

The Akwesasne experience in attempting to gain control over its judicial authority has been duplicated in many Native communities across North America. Indigenous leaders have determined that European-based legal systems simply don't work for Native people, and as a result there has been a reexamination of ancestral laws of reconciliation and compensation as alternative, preferable to imprisonment.

Support for a return to the traditional legal system will require teaching Native people how it would be applied, since Western laws have been predominant over the past few generations. Agreements would also have to be made with

Canada and the United States to respect Native jurisdiction in criminal and civil matters, an arrangement that could have considerable appeal given the enormous costs of external law enforcement and imprisonment.

NO EVADING NATURAL LAW

One of the principal foundations of American Indian reality was its recognition of a set of rules called natural law. Native philosophers recognized that all life on this planet followed certain rules, which, if adhered to, enabled a given species not only to survive but to reproduce and pass on its strongest genetic characteristics. Violation of natural law brought suffering, destruction, and death, a circumstance from which there was no appeal.

Life in most Native societies in pre-Columbian America tailored human reality to harmonize with nature; therefore, when Europeans began to colonize North America, they found a land free from contamination. One could travel from Massachusetts to California and find all waters free of pollutants, endless forests full of healthy wildlife, and air free of poisonous fumes. Some will argue there were many instances when Indian people deliberately sought to manipulate land and water to fit specific human designs, but no one disputes this continent was, in fact, paradise on earth.

In Iroquois society, one of the most serious of crimes was to despoil land or water to such an extent as to prevent its use, not only by people but by plants and animals as well. Traditional Iroquois did not believe any person had the right to claim possession or ownership of the earth, to do with it as he or she pleased. Individuals, families, clans, and nations had a right to occupy and use land, but only insofar as they cared for it in trust for the next generation.

This cardinal rule bound the Iroquois to a precise policy of careful resource management that included reforestation activities, strict hunting laws, and complex planting techniques meant to secure life while giving communal thanks for the earth's bounty.

Individual economic initiative was not something the Iroquois valued, since they knew it inevitably resulted in greed, envy, and the creation of an economic class system, leading in turn to the corruption of our political leaders as the wealthy sought to preserve their possessions. All the resources of the earth were to be shared in common and distributed according to need.

While this way of life worked well for the Iroquois for many generations, the past decade has been a bad one for ancestral Iroquois values. On every Iroquois reservation there has risen a so-called "business" class determined to use any and all means to secure maximum monetary profit.

Traditional Iroquois laws no longer have much authority, because our customs have been ignored by federal and state governments, our beliefs belittled by churches, and our history trivialized by the schools. It should surprise no one that some among us took advantage of this demoralization and legal vacuum to start businesses that are an affront to our ancient laws.

An example of the evisceration of Iroquois traditions is the proliferation of gas stations. On a single seven-mile stretch along Route 37, there are seventeen large gasoline stations dispensing millions of gallons of fuel each month. Very few of them have effective environmental controls, follow any kind of spillage guidelines, or are prepared to clean up the frequent overflows that have polluted the wells of many area homes. The profit motive is supreme. The fuel-station owners treat any mention of natural law and its consequences as the whining of unrealistic Iroquois dwelling in the mythical past. These station owners are acting in direct contradiction to ancestral natural law. It is not simply that they have failed to adhere to the rules of the community; they have led a direct assault upon the health and well-being of elders, women, children, and men.

Unlike their ancestors, modern Iroquois have been struck by cancers, diabetes, various skin diseases, birth defects, and chemical poisoning caused by the drinking of polluted waters and the consuming of animals heavily laden with known carcinogens. Poor diet and widespread substance abuse compound these problems.

However, we should no longer find convenient external scapegoats, but must take a hard look at what we are doing to our lands and the terrible legacy we shall leave for our children. Should we not recognize our errors and act swiftly to clean up our mess before we suffer even greater trauma?

The Iroquois as a whole must elect to implement and enforce stringent environmental laws to protect the earth. We cannot trust in the assurances of individual business owners; if we have learned no other lesson over the past decade it is that the power of greed will eclipse even the best intentions.

In the end, for better or worse, the laws of nature will prevail and restore balance. One way or the other.

VII

GOVERNMENT & SOVEREIGNTY

A Rich Heritage

Much has been written about the Haudenosaunee Confederacy, its founding, history, and traditions. For generations Iroquois historians have maintained that the democratic principles guiding the Confederacy have had a profound influence upon the development of popular government in the United States—an idea that has been severely criticized by some non-Native scholars and upheld by others.

It is apparent to us that the concepts of a true democracy did not come from Europe, since at no time in its history prior to the twentieth century did any nation on that continent grant universal suffrage to its citizens. True, political theorists such as John Locke and Karl Marx were advocates of popular representation, but a truly functioning democratic government free from class, ethnic, gender, or age restrictions simply did not exist.

The widely praised Greeks held two thirds of their people in a state of slavery and denied women the right to participate in the governmental process. Romans were simply barbarians with a higher command of technology. The Roman Senate was a debating club for the male elite that sustained its legislative excesses sustained by legions of serfs. Everywhere in Europe or Asia people were oppressed, exploited, and denied what we have come to regard as our basic human rights. It's a wonder that part of the world did not sink into the sea, so great was the human suffering.

When the doors of America were opened to immigration, millions elected to venture into the unknown in hopes of a better life. The uncertainties before them had to be better than the despair they were leaving behind.

In our Iroquois territory, they found the freedom they longed for. The Iroquois were one of the very few nations on earth to abide by a constitution that protects free speech, religious tolerance, the right of popular assembly, and the right of its citizens not only to participate in government but also to dissent from its policies.

An administration formed along exclusive gender lines was simply unacceptable to the true Iroquois, as was any governing agency dominated by a single individual. The Iroquois recognized the corrupting powers of politics, so they refused to permit the formation of oligarchies, however benevolent.

In the Iroquois state, all citizens had the right to be informed of the decisions of their leaders, the right to voice their opinions, and the absolute right to disagree. Iroquois laws made no distinction as to age; even children were assured their opinions would be taken seriously.

The Iroquois constitution, the Great Law of Peace, set rigid standards for leadership. Any man or woman who was considered for a position of power had to be of upright moral character, have a stable family life, and be fully prepared to live in a state of humility and simplicity. Iroquois leaders were prohibited from becoming enriched while serving in government.

Impeachment of leaders who violated the Great Law did occur, but not until the accused was permitted an opportunity to put up a defense before a people's assembly. If convicted, however, the representative was disgraced and forever banned from public office.

Iroquois governments could pass and enforce laws, but any legislation could be vetoed if there was sufficient public opposition. In all Iroquois councils were an equal number of male and female representatives. Title names were reserved for the fifty male rotiiane (chiefs), each of whom was empowered to govern at the local level as well as having a seat on the Grand Council of Haudenosaunee. Either group had the option of enjoining legislation by filibuster. Openness of government, with full public disclosure of all proposed rules, agreements, and regulations, was the people's right.

Authority in Iroquois society sprang not from the government but from the people and through the clans. The clans served as extended family, social services agency, religious body, and court of justice. Each Iroquois belonged to a clan, whether through birth or adoption.

The clans controlled immigration, residency, names, and marriages. Using ostracism or shame, the clan leaders disciplined individuals who violated communal laws. Since the Iroquois did not place a great deal of emphasis on material wealth and shared all resources in common, crimes against property were very rare. Iroquois society did permit execution under certain circumstances, such as for murder, but rather than the state determining the sentence, it was the victim's family who levied the punishment.

Each member nation within the Confederacy held exclusive jurisdiction over its own territories except in matters such as war, land cessions, and agreements with other nations that affected the Iroquois as a whole. The Grand Council, composed of fifty chiefs from all five of the original Iroquois nations, confirmed the titles of all chiefs upon the recommendation of the respective nations, but could refer the matter back to the national council for further debate if there were reasonable cause. The Grand Council met periodically to debate issues of common concern to all the Iroquois.

The Grand Council could intervene in the affairs of a member state if it held that nation was placing the Confederacy in peril by acting contrary to the welfare of the entire league, but its powers of intervention were qualified by the need to avoid violence. In times of extreme crisis, the Grand Council is empowered to hold a nation's status in trust, as it did for the Mohawk Nation Council after the Revolutionary War when the Mohawks were driven from their ancient homelands west of Albany.

With its capital at Onondaga, the Grand Council continues to meet as it has for many hundreds of years. There are many divisions within Iroquois society, however; some communities, such as Cattaraugus and Allegany, have split from the Confederacy.

Other divisions have been created by the imposition of governing bodies in competition with traditional governments. At Kahanawake, Kanehsatake, Tyendinaga, Wahta, Oshweken, Southwold, and Akwesasne, the Canadian government has attempted to replace traditional governments with the "band council" system. Band councils follow a ballot system and adhere to the provisions of the federal Indian Act. With the exception of Wahta and Tyendinaga, traditional councils continue to exist, however, and have commanded significant popular support, resulting in a move to return to the ancestral administrative systems.

Many of the current problems plaguing the Iroquois stem from these artificial divisions and Albany's policies of "divide and conquer." Yet despite these challenges the Iroquois love of democracy lives on, nourished by a heritage unique in the world.

THE POWER OF THE CONFEDERACY

In times now past, the Haudenosaunee Confederacy was a powerful entity whose actions had a profound effect on eastern North America. From the Great Lakes to the southern Appalachians, north to the Hudson Bay and east to the Atlantic Coast, the Grand Council of the Confederacy monitored and vigorously controlled Indian affairs while regulating trade and commerce for the benefit of its citizens.

Delegates from European powers such as France and England were sent to the Confederacy's capital at Onondaga to secure the friendship of the Iroquois League, because the survival of their respective colonies depended upon peaceful relations with the Natives. The Haudenosaunee, for their part, were well aware of the powerful impact of contact with the Europeans, politically and culturally, but especially in the area of economics.

Manufactured goods brought to America by the Europeans were eagerly sought after by Native people, who in return exchanged furs, corn, fish, tobacco, and other trade goods. By a combination of chance and design, the Iroquois Confederacy had exclusive authority over the waterways of the Mohawk and St. Lawrence Rivers, which were the main arteries into the American interior.

If any nation, company, or individual outside the Confederacy wished to use these rivers, they were assessed a tax consisting of a portion of their trade goods. In return the Iroquois were responsible for maintaining trails, granting hunting and fishing privileges, and permitting the use of its lands for camping.

As a society that believed in sharing the profits of labor and commerce in common, the Iroquois opposed the development of a capitalist class system based on individual gain. The Iroquois were led by practical politicians who realized the power of a dollar (or a pound sterling) and understood the need to regulate economic growth.

The Iroquois realized if they were to make intelligent decisions about any given issue, they must have accurate information. They came to rely heavily on an extensive communication network that encompassed every region east of the Mississippi.

Using ancient trails the Iroquois had long-distance runners carry messages throughout the region. These runners were carefully selected not only for their endurance but also for their ability to memorize the instructions and information given to them by their respective governments. Some of these messengers could run upwards of a hundred miles a day. When a matter was of particular concern, the Iroquois would use runners in relays, so that meant an event in Mohawk territory was known to the Senecas within two or three days.

The Iroquois extended their jurisdiction beyond the immediate homelands. Envoys, diplomatic parties, and trade delegates could be found on every major waterway during the spring, summer, and fall. The paddling songs of the Iroquois canoeists echoed across the Ohio, Tennessee, and Hudson rivers as they traveled on conducting the Confederacy's business.

Those who maintain the Iroquois did not have strong, effective national governments capable of responding to the issues of the day as well as administering extensive public programs are mistaken. There is simply no way the Haudenosaunee Confederacy could have survived the demands of the time without consistent management practices monitored by an inclusive bureaucracy.

As the Confederacy contemplates contemporary issues such as the regulation of commerce and the active supervision of public services, its leaders would do well to look back into a remarkable history and remember what their ancestors achieved.

IROQUOIS TREATY MAKING

All Iroquois treaties with the Europeans are based on a formal agreement entered into between the Mohawk Nation and the Netherlands in the second decade of the seventeenth century. This agreement is called the "Guswenta" or Two-Row Wampum by the Haudenosaunee, who consider it fundamental to all relations between Natives and their neighbors.

The Mohawks had encountered the Dutch some years after the explorer Henry Hudson sailed up the river that now bears his name. Hudson was searching for a water route to the Pacific Ocean that would enable him to reach the Orient.

Instead, he met Natives from many nations inhabiting an area defined by broad rivers, rolling hills, and fertile soils. Since Hudson was in the employ of the Dutch, he claimed the territory for that nation regardless of the aboriginal people living there.

When the Dutch decided to establish a trading post at the confluence of the Mohawk and Hudson rivers, they realized they would need the permission of the Mohawk Nation since the building site was within Mohawk territory. A representative of the Dutch was sent to the Mohawks, then numbering in the many thousands. Their principal communities lay a day's canoe paddling west of the proposed post. The Mohawks realized the importance of having the Dutch as trading partners and granted permission for the post, which was called Ft. Orange. The name was changed to Albany when the English secured control of the colony.

Determined to protect their lands and their status as a separate people, the Mohawks negotiated a treaty that was, according to Iroquois custom, affirmed by having it recorded in a large wampum belt, which has been preserved by the Iroquois to the present day. The wampum belt consists of beads sculptured from the shell of the quahog clam. Wampum, or *anakoha*, is considered sacred and not only is used to recall treaties and other important national events but is also employed in ceremonies.

The actual Guswenta belt has two parallel purple rows of wampum on a white background. The Iroquois maintain the belt depicts a river upon which two crafts are traveling, the Native in a canoe and the European in a ship. The paths never intersect, meaning the Europeans pledge never to force their customs and laws upon the Iroquois less the vessels collide and both are capsized. The Iroquois also cite Guswenta as a warning to those who would try the impossible and keep a foot in either craft.

Guswenta was passed on by the Iroquois across the generations and accepted by the English when they acquired the Dutch colony permanently in 1674. The concept of treaty making as both an integral part of Iroquois-European relations and as an affirmation of the status of the Haudenosaunee as distinct national entities continued throughout the colonial era.

Treaties establishing peace, or affirming trade, were entered into with England and France. Perhaps the most important of these was the agreement of September 1701, in Montreal, by which almost a century of hostilities were concluded with the French.

Despite treaty arrangements, the growing numbers of European immigrants into the Northeast resulted in a steady loss of land by the Natives. The result was friction and violence as the Native peoples resisted colonial encroachment. The Iroquois tried to resolve this by pressing the English government into negotiating a treaty that would prohibit the

selling of land by Natives to individuals or colonial governments without approval of the Crown. The Iroquois also
sought to establish a firm boundary that the settlers were prohibited from crossing.

The result was the 1768 Ft. Stanwix Treaty, a compact that
attempted to resolve Iroquois concerns but failed to stop the
theft of their land. The Iroquois entered into treaties with the
colonies in 1775 in a vain effort to stay neutral in what the
Iroquois saw as a civil war.

The Haudenosaunee were deeply affected by the American Revolution. Thousands of Iroquois were forcibly driven
from their homes as dozens of their towns were destroyed.
Although some Iroquois were able to remain neutral, others
fought on the side of the English, and hundreds were killed in
battle. The victorious Americans were hardly sympathetic to
the Iroquois and had already initiated plans to divide Iroquois territory into sections, which were then given to
military veterans or sold to land speculators.

The United States was prevented from dismissing the Iroquois altogether by conditions on the Midwestern frontier,
where Native leaders such as Tecumseh were organizing a
massive resistance to American intrusions. U.S. officials were
determined to keep the Iroquois from joining Tecumseh; hence
the decision was made to address some of the Iroquois concerns with the passage of the 1790 Federal Non-Intercourse
Act, which was designed to prohibit states from taking Indian
land without Congressional approval.

This law, which is a critical factor in current Iroquois land
claims, was bolstered by the 1794 Canandaigua Treaty, the
only formal agreement between the Iroquois Confederacy
and the United States. In Canandaigua, the United States
agreed to respect the territory of the Iroquois, while enacting
provisions for the remediation of disputes. All the Iroquois

nations, including the dispossessed Mohawks, sent representatives to the treaty signing at Canandaigua, which was acknowledged by the Confederacy through a large wampum belt called the "George Washington Belt."

Guswenta and Canandaigua are recalled by the Haudenosaunee whenever they meet with U.S. officials, and these treaties form the basis of the current Iroquois territorial claims. Canandaigua in particular is cited by the Confederacy as an admission by the United States of the Confederacy's status as a treaty-making power.

THE IROQUOIS GRAND COUNCIL

One of the more remarkable accomplishments of Native people in America is seen in the survival of their indigenous political systems despite hundreds of years of active, and at times brutal, suppression. The Hopi of Arizona, the Shoshone of Nevada, the Seminole of the Florida interior, and the Iroquois of central New York are governed in a manner consistent with their pre-Columbian past.

Widely praised for its strong democratic principles, the Iroquois Confederacy continues to exercise significant spiritual, psychological, and physical authority within the Seneca, Onondaga, Oneida, Cayuga, Mohawk, and Tuscarora nations. Formed many generations prior to the arrival of Europeans in America, the Iroquois Confederacy has proved to be one of the most durable institutions created by human beings. Its vision of a world free from wars and living in harmony with the natural world is as relevant today as it was when the Confederacy was created on the southern shores of Lake Onondaga.

When the Peacemaker called the Iroquois nations together for the first time, he used symbols to indicate the need for unity. He raised an arrow before the delegates and snapped it in half, showing how easy it was to split a nation apart. But when he bound five arrows together, the assembly saw how difficult it was to break the bundle. The arrows tied together, the prophet said, represented the strength through unity that the Iroquois Confederacy would bring.

Using these ancient symbols as a means of adhering to the traditional disciplines and procedures, the members of the Iroquois Confederacy continue to hold session at Onondaga in a forum called the Grand Council. The chiefs of the Grand Council have the mandate to debate issues of mutual concern and enact legislation binding upon all Iroquois citizens.

A session of the Grand Council may be called by any member nation upon the sanction of the Onondaga Nation, whose fourteen chiefs serve as an "upper house" within the Confederate system. The nation calling for a Council session must insure the issues to be addressed are relevant to the entire Confederacy and must not interfere with any ceremonial activity taking place in any of the territories. If the Onondagas agree a session of the Grand Council should be held, they will send strings of wampum by special envoys (called "runners") to each Iroquois nation, calling for them to meet at the Confederate capital at a set date.

The Oneida and Mohawk delegations to the Council are each composed of nine national chiefs. The Senecas send eight representatives, and the Cayugas, ten. When the Confederacy was formed, there were five member nations. The Tuscaroras entered the league 270 years ago and were placed among the Oneidas and Cayugas, through whom they speak.

A session of the Grand Council is begun when the Onondagas select a chief to recite the opening address, a prayer to the Creator through which the Iroquois people give collective thanks and are reminded of their responsibilities to the coming generations and the natural world. Some say it also creates a spirit of tranquillity among the chiefs and encourages patience, while fostering the spirit of compromise.

A chairperson insures the Council's business moves along in an orderly way. Referred to as Tadodaho, the chairperson is always from the Onondaga Nation. He introduces the agenda, insures the proper procedures are followed, and monitors legislation as it passes among the delegates.

Once an agenda is agreed upon, the debate begins. The Mohawk and Seneca chiefs caucus together on the north side of the longhouse with the Oneida, Tuscarora, and Cayuga chiefs together on the south side. The Onondagas are seated to the east, with the public observing the proceedings at the west end of the longhouse.

Issues are discussed first by the Mohawk-Seneca side of the house. If they reach an agreement they send the matter over to the Oneida-Tuscarora-Cayuga side for debate, clarification, and ratification. Upon agreement, they will return it to the Mohawk-Seneca for approval before submitting the legislation to the Onondagas for approval or rejection. The chiefs must strive for consensus on all issues. Any chief may delay or stop pending legislation by voicing opposition to the proposed law, but he must have good cause for doing so.

During the course of the debate, the chiefs may seek clarification by asking for public input. Throughout this process, the clanmothers of the nations are closely monitoring the flow of discussion, ready and willing to lend their advice or to take a chief aside if they feel the delegate is acting contrary to the wishes of his people. At various times the people will be given the opportunity to address the chiefs to seek redress of their concerns, but no private individual has the right to disrupt the orderly proceedings of the Council.

Since the Grand Council does not have a standing army or police force, it must rely upon voluntary compliance with its laws. There is a provision in the constitution of the Iroquois Confederacy that provides for the raising of a militia, but this has not been called upon since the American Revolution.

The Confederacy can, and does, periodically intervene in the affairs of its member nations if it has determined the rights of the Iroquois as a whole are being adversely affected or there is a problem regarding leadership that cannot be resolved locally. The Grand Council can appoint arbitrators to assist Iroquois citizens in arriving at solutions acceptable not only to the community but to the Confederacy as a whole.

Confederate chiefs can be formidable negotiators. For example, in 1990 when the Canadian army failed to open the Mercier bridge, which had been closed by the Kahanawake Mohawk people to protest the racist actions of the provincial police force, Confederate delegates not only succeeded in having the barricades removed but were also able to secure an agreement that restored peace to the community.

Now active worldwide, the chiefs of the Confederacy have traveled to many countries on their own passports in an effort to persuade all peoples to take seriously the needs of the next seven generations and beyond. The practices learned within the Grand Council serve them well in various human rights forums and have once again secured a place for the Iroquois in the affairs of the world, while addressing the concerns of the nations of the Confederacy.

IROQUOIS GOVERNMENT: HOW IT WORKS

There have been many questions raised with regard to how an Iroquois government works. While this information might have been at one time mainly of interest to non-Native anthropologists and historians, the growing importance of

Iroquois affairs to the residents of central New York makes a clear understanding of Iroquois government essential.

There are presently two types of administrative agencies on Iroquois reservations within New York State: elected, of which there are two, and traditional, which number six. The elected councils select representatives by popular vote using a secret ballot, in a system similar to that of the United States. These representatives hold office for a fixed number of years and are subject to various New York State laws regarding local officials.

Elected councils have no place within the Haudenosaunee. Should they have a matter to bring to the attention of the Grand Council, they must channel their concerns through a traditional government. Traditional councils at Tonawanda, Tuscarora, and Onondaga are recognized by the United States and New York State as the representatives of their respective nations.

Recognition by the United States enables a Native government to secure financial assistance and initiate land claims litigation; it also means both state and federal agencies are required to acknowledge its jurisdiction, however limited. Certain economic activities, such as commercial gambling and tobacco sales, are possible only with federal recognition. The Seneca reservations of Allegany and Cattaraugus south of Buffalo have a single governing body called the "Seneca Nation," which broke from the Iroquois Confederacy in 1848. It has its own constitution, court, and police systems. Seneca representation in the Haudenosaunee is through the Seneca Nation at Tonawanda (sometimes called the Tonawanda Band of Senecas).

The Cayugas are presently attempting to secure land within their ancestral territory around Cayuga Lake in Seneca and Cayuga counties, but they retain a traditional system in absentia, which is part of the Confederacy and legally protected under the 1794 Treaty of Canandaigua. They maintain their seat at the Grand Council from Cattaraugus, where they have resided since 1807. Their reservation west of Syracuse was lost as the result of two fraudulent "state" treaties in 1795 and 1807, both of which have been held by U.S. courts to be illegal, since Congress retains the exclusive power to alienate Native land. Many Cayugas have lived with the Senecas at Cattaraugus since they lost their homeland, while others moved to the Grand River (Oshweken) Reserve in Ontario or to northeastern Oklahoma.

The Oneida Nation of New York has a single representative to the Confederacy. It has two U.S. federally recognized "representatives," one who resides at Onondaga and another who oversees the activities of a group called the "Men's Council." This agency was created in 1993 over the objections of the Grand Council of the Haudenosaunee, which refuses to recognize its existence. The Men's Council government selected a group of women to act as counselors; these women are called "clanmothers." This designation was refuted by the Haudenosaunee, which acknowledges but one clanmother for the New York-based Oneidas. That single clanmother removed the Men's Council leader in 1995, an act that was ignored by the leader and the Council. The second federally recognized Oneida representative, residing at Onondaga, has not taken an active role in Oneida affairs.

A group of traditional Oneidas residing on the ancient homelands, called the Onyata:aka, have sought to replace the Men's Council by returning to the nine chiefs–nine clanmother system, but have met with considerable resistance.

The Oneidas of Wisconsin follow an elected "tribal council" system, while the Oneidas of Southwold, Ontario, have both traditional and elected governments. The elected, or band council, is the only one acknowledged by the Canadian authorities, which means the band oversees the administration of all federal assistance. The traditional council oversees the ceremonial and spiritual activities of the community. The Wisconsin Oneidas do not have a seat within the Confederacy, while the Southwold group does have limited representation.

The Onondaga Nation is the most stable of all Iroquois communities. It has a single governing agency, the Onondaga Nation Council of Chiefs and an active traditional ceremonial cycle overseen by the chiefs and clanmothers. Economic growth has been along culturally acceptable lines, although there was a period of conflict between individual entrepreneurs and the Nation in the early 1990s. The conflict was resolved with the expulsion of the business owners and the nationalization of the lucrative tobacco trade.

At Akwesasne, there are three governing bodies, only one of which is a member of the Haudenosaunee Confederacy. The situation of the Mohawk territory of Akwesasne is quite complicated. Divided in half by the international border, Akwesasne was until this century governed by a traditional Mohawk council, sometimes called the "life chiefs." In 1892, New York State created an entity called the St. Regis Tribal Council, which is legally a type of county government under state law. This Council holds annual elections on a rotating basis for three "chiefs" and three "sub-chiefs," along with a tribal clerk. Despite repeated attempts by the community to disband the Tribal Council, it is supported both financially and militarily by New York State. It is a matter of deep concern to the Confederacy that New York officials have elected to bypass the traditional democratic government and deal exclusively with this state agency with regard to such controversial matters as gambling, land claims, and policing.

The St. Regis Tribal Council has neither a constitution nor a justice system. The Tribal Council does not have treaty status and is therefore not a sovereign Indian government. It is not protected under the 1794 Treaty of Canandaigua, the 1796 Jay Treaty, or the 1784 Treaty of Ft. Stanwix, all of which define Native rights or recognize Iroquois independence; nor is it a part of the Iroquois Confederacy.

There is a similar elected council on the Canadian side of Akwesasne called the Mohawk Council of Akwesasne. It was created in 1899 by the Canadian government and imposed upon the Mohawks by force of arms. It is also elected, holding a popular vote every three years for twelve chiefs and one "grand chief." It has its own regulations and a justice system, but is not a member of the Confederacy.

The third governing agency at Akwesasne is the Mohawk Nation Council of Chiefs, a body of nine chiefs and nine clanmothers who hold office for life or until they are removed by their clans. The Mohawk Nation Council, as the traditional government, claims jurisdiction of all Akwesasne, although it lacks a financial base and has not secured the formal recognition of either Canada or the United States. It is, however, part of the Iroquois Confederacy.

Traditional Iroquois representatives must meet very specific qualifications before being considered as candidates for public office. Since they function as both civil and spiritual counselors, potential leaders must demonstrate knowledge of the ancient beliefs of the Iroquois. They must take active part in the many ceremonies held throughout the year and in fact are required to speak on behalf of their clans during these important events.

A candidate must also be married and demonstrate that he or she has taken good care of spouse and children. The Iroquois believe one who has failed to maintain a family adequately cannot be trusted with the well-being of the nation. If an individual has problems with alcohol or other substances, that person is excluded from office, since a leader must have a clear mind at all times. Since they represent their respective nations, candidates' behavior must be of the highest caliber. A candidate must be patient and willing to sacrifice time and possessions for the good of the people. A leader must not be enriched while in office but must maintain a humble lifestyle.

A candidate must also be of the clan that was inherited from his or her mother. There are nine Iroquois clans but not all nations have all clans. The Mohawks and Oneidas have three: Bear, Wolf, and Turtle. A candidate must be from one of these three, but it is possible for the clan members to "borrow" an Iroquois from another nation to hold office temporarily if they can find no one otherwise qualified within their own territory.

Perhaps the most important quality any Iroquois leader can have is a lack of personal ambition with regard to power and prestige. Iroquois customs dictate keeping power away from any individual who actively seeks it. There is no such thing as lobbying for office in Iroquois society; there are no declared candidates or primaries. The Iroquois distrust such aggressiveness, believing it leads to corruption and takes power away from the clans.

Candidates are nominated by the female leader of a clan, the clanmother. The clanmother may be a woman of any age but is usually an elder. Clanmothers are appointed for life by an assembly of the clan and are required to meet the same standards as the men. They do not have the authority to engage in any activity that affects the clan without its approval. This female leader selects male representatives to the national council, monitors their behavior, applies discipline when warranted, and upon serious breach of duty removes the male leader from his position as chief.

Once selected by the clanmother, a leadership candidate is brought before the clan for approval. All clan members have a right to express their support or rejection of the proposed leader, but if they are in opposition they must give good cause. If but one person is adamant in the belief that the candidate is unsuitable, then the nominee is considered rejected. Clan decisions can at times be laborious and lengthy, but approval of the candidate has to be unanimous.

If the candidate is approved by the clan by consensus, the nomination is passed on to a gathering of all the people. With each person sitting in their respective clan areas, the candidate is brought before a popular assembly. Again, if there is well-founded opposition, the candidate is forced to withdraw. If the people are in agreement, their decision is brought before the national council for approval. If approved, the candidate might serve on the national council as an assistant chief with limited duties.

Finally, the candidate is required to go through a ritual called the Condolence Ceremony before the Grand Council. This involves the formal installation of the candidate as a chief of the Iroquois Confederacy through an ancient and sacred rite for which all the leaders of the Confederacy are assembled. The Confederate representatives have the option of withholding recognition by refusing to conduct the ceremony, but this has very rarely happened.

During the ceremony the candidate is again reminded of his duties to the people under the Great Law of Peace. He is considered as officially sworn into office when a set of deer antlers is placed upon his head. From that moment on he holds one of the fifty Iroquois Confederacy title names given to the original representatives when this first League of Nations was formed nearly a thousand years ago.

Being a Confederate chief is an exhausting and demanding position. It requires great patience and diplomatic finesse. A chief hears many complaints and is expected to serve as a wise and impartial arbitrator. All his actions are closely monitored by the clanmothers and the people. At the same time, the clans are expected not to burden the chiefs unduly with minor complaints and are to provide for the well-being of him and his family while he is attending to the nation's affairs.

Iroquois chiefs are prohibited from engaging in acts of violence and do not have the right to declare war. They are "peace" leaders, and they must do everything in their power to achieve reconciliation. They do not possess the authority to sign any agreement or engage in any activity that affects the clan without full clan approval. They must speak on behalf of the clan before the Grand Council, when the chiefs of the Iroquois Confederacy meet.

It is the obligation of his clanmother to act as the conscience of a rotiiane, to remind him of his duties and, when warranted, to apply discipline. If, after repeated warnings, the rotiiane does not modify his wayward actions, the clanmother removes him from office. As a sign of their office, the clanmothers hold a special string of wampum beads.

There is no greater shame in Iroquois society than to have one's antlers (or "horns") removed for violating the trust of the people. For committing such an act, the chief is expelled from office. In Iroquois terms, the removal of the antlers causes the former chief to figuratively bleed from his forehead until the day he dies. The disgrace is so severe that the ousted man is shunned by all Iroquois and considered the "walking dead."

In Iroquois law if any of its member nations does not have the means to continue as an independent state, its status is held in trust by the Grand Council until such a time as that nation is once again in a position to function as a full member of the Confederacy. The formal recognition process is called "having a council fire."

After the American Revolution, the Mohawks were forced to flee their homelands in the Mohawk Valley and its "fire" (or nation status) was given to the Grand Council for preservation. Over a hundred years passed before the Mohawks of Akwesasne were formally recognized as an independent Mohawk Nation Council and were able to resume their position with the Grand Council.

A similar occurrence took place around 1830, when a majority of the Oneidas left central New York for Wisconsin and Canada. It was up to the Grand Council to watch over the interests of the Confederacy as a whole. The Oneidas remaining in New York maintained a national identity while living at Onondaga or in other communities including their small holdings in Madison County. Throughout this time, the Oneidas have sustained representation on the Grand Council, but await a formal return of their council fire to their original territory.

Since the Revolutionary War, the Oneidas have attempted to overcome the cultural devastation caused by extreme land loss and economic depression. So serious was the threat to their survival that many Oneidas decided the only way open to them was to leave this region. The state of New York bears an enormous responsibility for this tragedy, since its policies of signing illegal land cession deals with unauthorized ethnic Oneidas resulted in millions of acres of Oneida land being stolen from beneath their very feet. Amidst great suffering, Oneidas fled to Wisconsin and Ontario, but never lost hope that one day some of them would return. This dream of territorial and monetary compensation for their pain is the basis for the Oneida claims against New York.

The Oneidas secured a major victory in 1985 when they won a land claims case in the U.S. Supreme Court. The Court held New York State did not have the authority to enter into treaties with the Iroquois and decided the Oneidas held title to 235,000 acres of their original 3-million-acre territory. Negotiations to reach a settlement, carried on for over fifteen years, raised some serious problems, however. In February 2000, the Oneida Nation of New York, an entity recognized by the U.S. federal government but not the Haudenosaunee, attempted to exclude the Oneidas of Southwold, Ontario, from a settlement proposal. The proposal would have provided $500 million to the Oneidas of New York and Wisconsin. The Oneida Nation of New York would have ceded its claim to most of the 235,000 acres of the original Oneida homeland in exchange for the right to use slot machines and sell alcohol in its Turning Stone Casino—an offer that enraged the Southwold Oneidas.

There are now approximately 1,100 Oneida Nation members in central New York with thousands of others in Ontario and Wisconsin. The rapid economic growth of the Oneidas in this region has only contributed to the complexity of an issue felt by every resident of central New York.

But it is the Oneidas themselves who must determine if the Great Law is applicable to their lives and if its leadership will be selected according to its provisions in a free, open, and democratic forum. Their decision will determine the status of the Oneida Nation within the Iroquois Confederacy. This choice is not the prerogative of the state or federal government, or leaders of other Confederate nations. It is up to the Oneida people to decide their collective fate and to do so hopefully in harmony with the ancient traditions of the Iroquois Confederacy.

TAXES VIOLATE OUR TREATIES

Does New York State have the authority to ignore U.S. federal law in its aggressive attempts to collect taxes from Iroquois citizens?

Since the 1980s, New York Department of Taxation and Finance officials have waged war against the tax-free status of the Iroquois, even to the point of collecting revenues on territory that has been determined by the U.S. government to be clearly Native. For example, the land upon which the Carousel Mall was built (on the southern shore of Onondaga Lake, just off Interstate 81 in Syracuse, New York) is located within the borders of the Onondaga Nation. This area was leased to New York but was never ceded by the Onondagas; hence it remains under Onondaga Nation jurisdiction. Yet New York has held that most purchases made by Iroquois citizens at the Carousel Mall, among other places, must be taxed and has ordered area merchants to reject Iroquois claims of tax immunity.

State officials have attempted to place other restrictions on what an Iroquois may, or may not, buy. Items that are tax exempt must, according to the state, be delivered to the purchaser's reservation home by either the United Parcel Service or the U.S. Post Office. Since when, the Iroquois counter, did the Department of Taxation and Finance have the authority to define Native land or to determine how a product is to be delivered? Iroquois shoppers have been placed in the unenviable position of having to debate this issue with uninformed clerks while standing in the checkout line, often with other people standing impatiently behind them.

When this issue, which involves treaties and U.S. Supreme Court decisions, is brought to the attention of the store managers, they claim they are only responding to the directives of the state tax agents, who have told them that any unpaid tax on a product sold to a Native outside of the tight restrictions will be assessed against the store. Officials within the Department of Taxation and Finance have not responded to requests to discuss this issue. These public servants have been described as "away from the office," or have temporarily "stepped out," or been busy on phone calls discussing issues of supposed greater importance.

Almost without exception, the current territorial boundaries of the seven Iroquois reservations were set by New York State in a series of land transactions that have been held by the U.S. Supreme Court to be illegal, since the state never possessed the authority to expropriate Indian land. By treaty, Iroquois territory at its minimum includes 250,000 acres in Oneida-Madison counties; 64,000 acres around Seneca Falls; 9 million acres of Mohawk lands; 6 million acres belonging to the Senecas; and 2.6 million acres constituting the homeland of the Onondagas. By law, New York State must acknowledge the tax-free rights of the Iroquois within these regions.

Chief Irving Powless of the Onondaga Nation has led a decades-long fight to remove these arbitrary restrictions on the tax-free state of the Iroquois. Powless asks by what authority New York State qualifies the rights of the Iroquois. Powless says there is no federal statute or treaty provision that restricts the tax-free status of the Iroquois to a reservation, and under the Jay Treaty, the Native people are clearly exempted from highway tolls and assessments of any kind on their goods.

Rather than being upset with this exemption, Powless remarks, the people of New York State should consider the enormous wealth they have derived from Iroquois land and contrast it with the pittance state tax officials are trying to extract from Native families.

As Powless states, U.S. courts have ruled that treaties must be interpreted as the Native people understood them at the time of signature. The Iroquois of seven generations ago were determined to remain free from all U.S. taxes, a stance that has never wavered despite the opposition of New York State.

GAMBLING WITH SOVEREIGNTY

Opposition to gambling in Iroquois society is deeply rooted, going back almost two hundred years, to the time when prophet Handsome Lake delivered a message from the spirit world forbidding the Iroquois from becoming involved in games of chance. The spiritual beings informed Handsome Lake he was to bring to the Iroquois a set of moral rules to guide the people through the difficult times of change that would be their lot for the forseeable future. The Seneca preacher passed on their prediction that turmoil would tear apart the Iroquois if they ignored his message.

The Haudenosaunee Confederacy has warned other indigenous groups to be cautious about taking this economic development route, not only because it violates traditional Iroquois law but it also inevitably results in the diminishing of aboriginal sovereignty for short-term gain.

The Confederacy's advice was brushed aside, with predictable results. Those Iroquois councils that have signed gambling compacts have no choice but to acknowledge the policing powers of New York, cede taxing authority to the federal government, and grant U.S. courts unqualified powers to interfere in the lives of their people. In addition, the U.S. federal courts have held the states have the right to full consultation in the Native gambling process. They must also be a party to any agreements between the U.S. federal government and the Native nations, which amounts to the states' holding veto power over such contracts if they deem them contrary to their interests.

Opponents to gaming knew it caused as many social ills as it cured. Traditional Iroquois leaders have long argued money alone cannot solve a community's problems, especially in a time of spiritual crisis, social transition, and cultural and linguistic loss. They have said gaming is such a powerful force it must be handled with extreme caution and should be permitted only when a community has had time to prepare for the radical changes it will bring about.

With gaming come increased demands upon natural resources and social services along with compromises in Native jurisdiction, sovereignty, and law enforcement. Gaming also brings additional state controls and ultimately leads to the taxation of Iroquois income by both the United States and New York. For some Iroquois the lure of easy wealth was too strong to resist.

Gaming began on the Akwesasne territory in 1984 and with it a protracted battle to determine the fate of the Mohawk people. The bitter experiences of the Mohawks have been repeated in every Iroquois community where gaming has been promoted as the cure for economic and social ailments. Cattaraugus, Tuscarora, Oshweken, Kahanawake, Kanehsatake, Oneida and Onondaga have been rocked by disputes over gaming.

The reality of casino operations does not always meet the expectations of the casino operators. The casino at Akwesasne has proven to be less of a success than hoped for, as potential customers have been drawn to gambling dens in Hull, Quebec, and nearby Montreal. The casino operators have had to answer charges of raw sewage being dumped into the St. Regis River and the ongoing contamination of the reservation's groundwater from construction connected with the building of the gambling facility. Actions against the casino were filed with the U.S. Environmental Protection Agency.

Advocates for the expansion of casino gambling in New York have also attempted to have the St. Regis Tribal Council convert the Monticello Race Track in the Catskills to a casino. Opponents argue the land in consideration is outside of the aboriginal territory of the Mohawks and would require a special act by the U.S. Department of the Interior to place it in trust status, a tactic that has been defeated in the Midwest.

There are many alternatives to gaming. Iroquois leaders have been meeting with federal and state representatives on a trade and commerce agreement that will eliminate the threat of state taxation while giving Native governments exclusive control over their local economies. This will mean each reservation business will be subject to Iroquois regulations, with the greater portion of the profits going to the community rather than enriching a few individuals.

Iroquois Confederacy leaders foresee enterprises such as the marketing of organic foods, arts and crafts, and the creation of free trade zones as options for growth other than gaming. These plans will take some time before they bear fruit and will require plenty of work, but the ultimate benefit will be a healthier Iroquois people enhanced by a strong work ethic and a way of life in harmony with our ancestral values.

IROQUOIS AT THE UNITED NATIONS

For decades, Native leaders have been knocking at the doors of the United Nations, trying to gain admittance so they can make their arguments for admission as sovereign states, an idea the United States adamantly opposes. Several Native nations, such as the Hopi, Shoshone, and the members of the Haudenosaunee Confederacy maintain they have never ceded their independence to the United States. They point to a long history as nations, a tradition recognized by the United States when it entered into treaty relationships with their governments.

Instead, U.S. courts have declared Indians to be members of "dependent" nations who occupy their lands at the pleasure of Congress, a political body that may at any time elect to abrogate Native status altogether.

In other words, Indians have no rights Congress is legally bound to respect.

Having opposed this concept for generations, the leaders of the Haudenosaunee have tried to have their case heard before the United Nations. In 1977, they succeeded in gaining recognition as a "non-government organization" (or NGO) at the U.N. human rights assembly in Geneva, Switzerland, but this action was without teeth. The Haudenosaunee would not give up the fight, which they believe will one day result in Iroquois delegates taking their rightful place among the community of nations.

Iroquois leaders can point to some successes in the last eighteen years that give them considerable cause for hope. They were granted standing before the Fourth Russell International Tribunal held in Holland in 1984. This entity, composed of judges and legal scholars from throughout the world, provides a forum for disadvantaged peoples to plead their cases.

The Iroquois did so, presenting a long list of human rights abuses suffered at the hands of the United States. Given the strength of the Iroquois case, the Tribunal found it relatively simple to condemn the American government for its longstanding policy of suppressing indigenous people.

In 1984, the Confederacy participated in an international assembly of Native peoples in Panama and there helped draft a "Declaration of Principles of Indigenous Rights." Iroquois delegates returned to Geneva in 1989 to persuade the United Nations' General Conference of the International Labour Organization to move to protect Native societies against being exploited by land- and resource-hungry governments and corporations.

Confederacy speakers were also present at the Earth Environmental Summit in Rio de Janeiro, Brazil, in 1992 and lobbied for the decision by the United Nations to declare 1993 the "International Year of the Indigenous Peoples."

The hard work of the Haudenosaunee on behalf of the world's Native populations has won for them many friends at the United Nations. It therefore came as no surprise when the United Nations Environmental Programme agreed to hold a one-day session at U.N. headquarters in New York City to listen to the Iroquois concerns about the ongoing contamination of their ancestral homelands.

On July 18, 1995, official representatives from all member nations (with the exception of the Oneidas of New York, who elected not to participate) came to the United Nations to give testimony about conditions in Iroquois territory. They identified environmental degradation and territorial displacement as the primary causes of the internal tensions that has plagued the Confederacy for over a decade.

Removed from their lands by force and fraud, the Iroquois suffered through adverse economic and social conditions that resulted in social chaos and political unrest. From the industrial pollutants that have destroyed farming and fishing at Akwesasne to the inundation of Allegany by the Kinzua Dam, the Iroquois have come perilously close to extinction as a distinct people because their traditional economies based on their natural resources were undermined. It should shock no one, the Haudenosaunee argued, that given poverty and lack of viable economic opportunities, many Iroquois have turned to criminal activities to make a living, with further adverse effects on the environment.

But the Haudenosaunee are not ones to simply complain. Working in conjunction with Cambridge University in

England, the Environmental Protection Agency, Indigenous Development International, as well as the United Nations itself, the Confederacy submitted a report entitled "Haudenosaunee: Environmental Restoration—An Indigenous Strategy for Human Sustainability."

This document summarizes the current conditions on Iroquois lands and offers concrete solutions to return Mother Earth to her former state. It proposes the creation of an indigenous environmental learning center to study problem areas and offer solutions. This center would also coordinate information, define economic development strategies and assist in the preservation of culture.

The Confederacy pledged itself to raising at least $26 million over the next five years for the project while seeking the assistance of the United Nations, which in turn might use this concept to assist Native peoples worldwide.

Haudenosaunee representatives such as Oren Lyons, Henry Lickers, Dennis Bowen, Leo Henry, Audrey Shenandoah, Jake Swamp, Leon Shenandoah, Charles Wheelock, Clint Halftown, Carol Jacobs, and Bernie Parker were applauded by U.N. Undersecretaries Richard Butler and Keith Johnson for their perseverance, dedication, and creativity in arriving at an equitable solution to a very difficult problem.

While the Haudenosaunee Confederacy might be years away from entering the United Nations as a nation, its presence before environmental and human rights forums as the most outspoken advocate for indigenous peoples from throughout the hemisphere makes admission a stronger possibility for the near future.

VIII

IROQUOIS LEADERS

IROQUOIS HEROES

In the traditions and legends of any society there are heroes
and villains whose stories define the spiritual and cultural
values of a people. The Iroquois have epics telling how the
world was formed, how human beings were brought forth
from the mud of the earth, and how the Haudenosaunee
Confederacy was created.

There is Aientsik the Skywoman, the first human-like
being to walk on this land. She came from a land beyond the
stars, descending from the heavens on a beam of pure light.

Aientsik gave birth to Tekawerahkwa, a daughter whose
father is called Taronhiawakon, the Holder of Heavens. In
time Tekawerahkwa had two children, the twins Tawiskaron
and Okwiraseh.

It is said Tawiskaron was a mischievous being whose
skin was as hard as flint. He was greatly jealous of his
brother, who went about the earth creating all that is beautiful and good. Tawiskaron tried to imitate his twin but
could not. When Okwiraseh made the powerful eagle,
Tawiskaron could only form the bat; if the good twin
formed smooth-flowing rivers, his brother threw in rocks
to make dangerous rapids.

As Iroquois, we are told the two finally met in a battle in
which Okwiraseh was the victor. Tawiskaron was confined to
the dark regions of the earth, where he rules the night and

creatures so terrible that to look upon them would result in immediate death.

In time, the Iroquois came to be like an extended family, but then they grew apart. An era of great troubles divided the Iroquois into hostile factions marked by violence and terror. It was during these grim days that the Peacemaker arrived in our territory form the Northwest. Believed to be a divine being, the Peacemaker was sent by the Creator to persuade the Iroquois to abandon war and form a League of United Nations that would stand for all the world to see as an example of how humans might live in peace.

This remarkable god-man was assisted in his work by an orator named Aiionwatha (Hiawatha) and Jikonsasay, the first woman to embrace the Great Law of Peace. Because of her support of his efforts, the Peacemaker gave Iroquois women considerable power within the Confederacy. There was also Tadodaho, the grand wizard of the Onondagas, who was given the chairmanship of the Grand Council of the Confederacy. Said to have had snakes woven in his hair and a body marked by bends in seven places, Tadodaho was the last but certainly the most powerful leader to join the League.

In the historical period, the Iroquois have had many heroes they may rightfully take pride in.

Garakontie was the most respected Iroquois leader from 1650 to 1678. An Onondaga, he was a firm advocate of peace. He met with the Dutch, English, and French along with many Native nations in his capacity as an ambassador for the Confederacy.

The Cayuga chief Ourhouasse was imprisoned by the French and sent to Europe, where he labored as a slave in a galley ship for two years before returning to Iroquois territory in 1689.

Onkiswathetami, or Shikellamy, was active among the Iroquois during the first decade of the 1700s. He was born a French Canadian, but was granted citizenship among the Oneidas. He played a key role in forming an alliance between the Confederacy and Pennsylvania in 1736. Thereafter, he served as the Confederacy's delegate to the Native peoples in that region.

Among the Mohawks, a great hero was Hendrick, or Teoniahigarawe. He was selected by the Mohawk Nation to travel to England in 1710 to visit Queen Anne. He served as a military commander among the Mohawks, played a key role in the 1754 Albany Conference, and was killed defending the Confederacy at the age of seventy-five during the 1755 Battle of Lake George.

Tanaghrisson was called the "Half King" among the Native people of the Ohio and Kentucky regions. He was a Catawba by birth but was naturalized a Seneca. He was sent by the Confederacy to oversee its protectorate lands in the Midwest and served as an advisor to George Washington before dying in 1754.

Old Smoke, or Kaienkwaahton, was a Seneca leader during the critical times before, during, and after the American Revolution. He was a great fighter who helped plan the American defeat at Oriskany in 1777, as well as conducting the attacks against the Wyoming Valley. He died in 1786, still an opponent of the United States.

A compatriot of Old Smoke was Kiyasuta, another Seneca military leader. He assisted the French when they defeated the English general Braddock in 1755 and later lent aid to Pontiac in his war with Great Britain. He also fought the Americans during the Revolution in defense of his people.

These leaders serve as reminders to the Iroquois of their remarkable history as well as examples of loyalty, dedication, and bravery we would all do well to emulate.

NOT ALL LEADERS WERE HEROES

He had risen to a position of unparalleled power and authority. He was courted by the political elite, and his advice was sought on matters of great importance. In his homeland, nothing could be done without his approval. In time he grew to believe he was chosen by God to lead his people—despite their reluctance.

The leader was given access to formal education and placed in the best schools. He learned to appreciate the demands of his instructors. He mastered his courses, impressing his teachers with his unwavering ambition to do what none of his kind had ever done before.

He dreamt of a great international alliance, of a political state so powerful it would command the attention of the world. He would be its leader and raise his people to great heights of influence and wealth, despite their own misgivings.

At times, it seemed to him his own community was overly doubtful. He sensed mistrust even within his immediate family, but he would permit neither subtle criticism or quarrel to dissuade him from acting as he thought best. Given their embarrassing habit of speaking their minds, he kept his relatives at a distance, preferring to socialize with those who shared his values and could articulate their thoughts with an equal degree of passion.

He viewed the pagan practices of his Iroquois kin with disdain. It was their privilege to worship nature by dancing in circles and chanting ancient songs. He believed such activities could only act as a brake on progress and prevent the Iroquois from taking advantage of their economic opportunities. He knew the world had little patience for those who refused to recognize changing times; it would be best for all if the pagan party took heed of the latest political and social developments and adapted to them.

As a leader, he was not deeply religious, preferring not to trivialize his feelings by public displays of emotions of the kind common within the longhouse. As an Anglican, he believed in the European god because it got results. It was the deity of business and industry, the god of aggression and direct action: the preferred model, in his mind, of a supreme being.

The traditional songs and dances did have their place, however, especially when he needed to impress his non-Native friends. They were always eager to see the Indians in "savage" dress. At the same time, he felt slightly chagrined whenever he had to call upon the dancers, for it served to remind him of a heritage he would have preferred to cast aside. He did take great comfort in having made the conversion from barbarism to civilization and holding onto his material possessions as if they were his key to enter established society.

Cultivated by the powerful elite and given every vestige of authority, this Mohawk leader did exactly as he was trained to do. Called Joseph Brant by the British, he used his intellectual talents to challenge the power of the Haudenosaunee Confederacy and almost succeeded in destroying this great League.

Brant was selected by Sir William Johnson, the colonial superintendent of Indian affairs and one of the most powerful men in colonial America, to serve the interests of the British government by undermining the Confederacy, which, in the 1770s, was impeding the westward expansion of the colonies.

Receiving years of formal instruction at a private school in Connecticut, Brant returned to Mohawk territory determined to serve his English masters and to carve for himself a place in history. He adopted all the mannerisms of English nobility, from becoming a devout Christian to imitating their precise speech patterns.

It was Brant who pushed and prodded the Iroquois into war, taking every advantage of the political unrest during that time to promote the British cause. For his efforts, he was commissioned a captain in the British army and led one of the most effective military units of the Revolutionary War.

When challenged by the traditional chiefs of the Mohawk Nation, he simply brushed them aside, using his extensive political connections to assume dictatorial powers over the Mohawk people. It was Brant who provoked the U.S. military into invading Mohawk territory, and when the people were forced to flee their ancestral homes, Brant determined who received food and shelter.

Despite the best efforts of the Mohawk Nation to preserve the peace and remain neutral, Brant simply pushed the civil chiefs aside and began a six-year campaign of terror and destruction in central New York State.

The loss of Mohawk territory in New York (with the exception of a small reservation along the St. Lawrence River) was the direct result of Brant's alliance with the British. The victorious Americans, particularly veterans of the Continental Army, were in a vengeful mood after the war and had no sympathy for Haudenosaunee sovereignty.

After the war, it was Brant who led Iroquois refugees from all of the Six Nations into Canada and then began to sell the lands reserved for their use. With his profits, Brant constructed a mansion on the shores of Lake Ontario, where, it is said, he had black slaves serve his English visitors while dispirited Mohawks put on "scalp" dances for the entertainment of his guests.

Never given the title of chief by the Mohawk people, Brant nonetheless signed a "treaty" in 1797 that surrendered millions of acres of Mohawk land to the United States for $1,600 in travel money. Afterwards, he tried to form his own league of Native nations in the Midwest, but failed because his reputation for corruption was so widespread. He was held in such hatred that he could go nowhere without a contingent of bodyguards.

Brant also acted as a "land agent" for the Iroquois refugees when they were given land along the Grand River in western Ontario. He made extensive "gifts" of the reservation to his English friends while enriching himself. From an original grant in the millions of acres, the Iroquois of the Six Nations Reserve were left by Brant with a land base of but a fraction of what they once had.

Brant is held up by the Mohawk people today as an example of individual ambition and greed running contrary to Iroquois traditions. There are supposed to be brakes within Iroquois society that prevent the rise of individuals with powers such as Brant had, but these disciplines had broken down during a time of great stress. While Brant may have died over 180 years ago, it is the Mohawk people who today suffer the effects of his leadership even as they loathe the man.

Condemned to life on a small, heavily polluted reservation in northern New York, the Mohawk Nation Council of Chiefs is trying desperately to overcome the terrible effects of Brant's leadership during and after the American Revolution. Hopes remain high that the traditional, peace-loving Mohawk people might soon return to their ancestral homelands along the Mohawk River.

A resettlement site has been tentatively selected near Canajoharie which, by no coincidence, was the community of Joseph Brant. With luck, and the active support of the citizens of New York, the Mohawks and other Haudenosaunee people might yet recover from the influence of Joseph Brant.

HANDSOME LAKE'S VISIONS SAVED THE IROQUOIS

There have been times in Iroquois history when the survival of the People of the Longhouse has been in doubt. Both external and internal forces have in the past driven the

Iroquois to the point of despair, but somehow they manage to survive.

According to oral tradition, the formation of the Iroquois Confederacy occurred as a result of the people's desire for radical change in their society. Violence, warfare, crime, and poverty were so common as to be the normal order of life.

While most Iroquois would have wished for a better way of life, the spiritual, political, and social revolution so desperately needed did not come about until the arrival of the Peacemaker. This man of God completely changed the course of Iroquois history by uniting the people under the Great Law of Peace and giving what had been a factionalized society a common sense of purpose.

Echoes of the Peacemaker's work live on throughout the world. It is said the founders of the American nation over two hundred years ago first learned the practical applications of democracy from the Iroquois. It is also true such political philosophers as Karl Marx and Freidrich Engels read about the Iroquois and were sufficiently impressed to refer to the Haudenosaunee as the ideal pre-technological communistic state they would have liked all humans to emulate. Our prophet was an advocate for universal peace, which was to be monitored by a world government founded upon democratic traditions and guided by respect for the natural world.

The powerful words of the Peacemaker have at times been obscured by collective and individual tragedies. As profane, complex, and intemperate beings, we have all too often fallen short of his standards. Our sense of urgency often will not permit us the time we need for reflection upon the subtleties of the Great Law or how its provisions might be applied to the problems at hand.

No one doubts the Iroquois are in a state of crisis. We continue to face many stresses in the new millennium. With problems ranging from the temptations of material wealth to the corruption of our youth, our communities are in grave danger of disintegration.

Crisis, however, is nothing new for the Iroquois. The last time we were in a similar situation was two hundred years ago, when our lands were stolen, our governments undermined, and our people spiritually broken. At that time, alcohol provided escape in the same way that now our young people resort to using crack cocaine. Murder, arson, and familial abuse were commonplace. We were adrift; our lives were without meaning.

It was at this juncture the Creator intervened to send another prophet. Unlike the Peacemaker, who was born of a virgin and was a performer of miracles, this messenger was a drunkard, perhaps one of the worst. Yet he was also a leader of the people and held the title of Skaniatariio (pronounced Ska-nia-da-li-yo), or Handsome Lake, as a representative of the Seneca Nation. He was of the Turtle Clan, born about the year 1735, and a veteran of the Revolutionary War. The war experiences had been generally bad for the Iroquois since they had fought well only to be abandoned by their British allies and left to the mercy of the vengeful Americans.

Skaniatariio shared the impotent rage of his nation when their territory was reduced to a few meager reservations. He took to drink and witnessed firsthand the terrible effect rum had on Native people. He spent decades on the bottle before being struck by an illness that left him an invalid for four years.

Near the end of this illness, Skaniatariio went into a coma. His relatives could find no sign of a pulse or breathing and believed he was dead. They were preparing his body for burial when Skaniatariio returned to consciousness with a message that would save the Iroquois.

Skaniatariio told the people of his "death" and rebirth. He spoke of the four sacred messengers who had come to visit him while he was between worlds. They gave him a set of teachings, which he was to share with the Iroquois.

Central to Skaniatariio's Good Words was the continuation of the ancestral rituals of thanksgiving and the abstinence from any substance that obscured the good mind. Skaniatariio told of the punishments in the afterlife that awaited those who abused spouses, committed acts of violence, or acted against the best interests of the people. He spent years traveling around Iroquois territory in an effort to halt the slide into chaos. He sought nothing less than a revolution within Iroquois society, as well as a way by which the Iroquois could live in peace with the Americans.

Skaniatariio preached about the need to preserve the family. He stressed the importance of caring for all children, the permanence of marriage, and the need to refrain from sexual promiscuity. He was concerned about the elders and told the Iroquois the Creator had forbidden any ill treatment of the aged.

Realizing the harm gossip causes in society, Skaniatariio spoke against idle tongues. He was opposed to land sales, stressed communal repentance, and taught the people how to adjust to changing times.

Skaniatariio also gave the Iroquois a set of prophecies. He anticipated the problems of our own era, when the Iroquois would again be placed under siege by their own kind. By adhering to the Good Word, he said, the Iroquois might survive to witness the purification of the planet by a fire of undetermined origin.

Skaniatariio died at Onondaga in 1815. In his lifetime, his teachings provoked considerable controversy, which continues on to the present day. Yet no one argues that, had it not been for the visions of this remarkable Seneca man, the Iroquois would surely have disappeared from this region long ago.

SAM GEORGE, ONONDAGA PATRIOT

Every contemporary Iroquois person takes some degree of meaning, and many a hefty dose of pride, in their identity as aboriginals and as the descendants of a great people who once controlled the destiny of a continent. Leaders of the Haudenosaunee Confederacy, however, have been criticized for their adherence to the traditional values that have preserved Iroquois identity. Others, most particularly the "progressive" elements within the Native communities, have accused the longhouse chiefs of frustrating development by refusing to change to fit modern times. The conflict between the traditional and the "modern" is not a new one.

The Iroquois have been gifted from time to time with remarkable leaders who have been able to give inspiration to their people by actively battling the insidious forces of assimilation and compromise. One such leader was an Onondaga by the name of Samuel George.

Mr. George was born about the year 1795 and passed into the spirit world in 1873. In his youth he was acknowledged as a long-distance runner without parallel. Following the ancient Iroquois trails, he carried messages from village to village, covering hundreds of miles in a matter of a few days.

George was also a military veteran, having fought in the War of 1812. He was a student of Handsome Lake, the remarkable Seneca prophet whose visions were so powerful as to literally save the Confederacy during a time of violence and despair. George took an active role in opposing attempts by Christian missionaries to convert Iroquois children, believing there was no reason to become other than what they were.

George was a critic of the controversial Buffalo Creek treaties of 1838 and 1842, when bribes were freely spread about by U.S. agents eager to possess the reservation and drive the Iroquois to Kansas and Oklahoma. When the traditional Iroquois lost their fight to hold onto Buffalo Creek, the Onondagas there returned home to their community south of Syracuse. Here they maintained the ancient rituals.

Sam George took an active role. He was cited by the Onondaga Nation as a leader when they appointed him Keeper of the Wampum, the official who was entrusted with the care and preservation of some of the most sacred possessions of the Confederacy. As Keeper, George was also expected to serve as an historian of the Iroquois. His considerable intellectual talents were devoted to the reading of the wampum belts, a recitation that takes many days to complete.

As a staunch supporter of the Confederacy, George opposed the decision by the Senecas of Cattaraugus and Allegany in 1848 to separate from the League and create a governing entity called the Seneca Nation of New York under the laws of New York State.

The U.S. government gave Samuel George the honorary rank of general during the Civil War for his efforts on behalf of the Haudenosaunee Confederacy. In November 1863, George met with U.S. President Abraham Lincoln to remind him of the American obligations under the 1794 Canandaigua Treaty: namely, to acknowledge the Iroquois as citizens of their own nations. In addition, George won the release of a number of Iroquois from U.S. military service.

Undoubtedly George's talent as traditional healer served him well within the community, as did his ability as an orator, a skill held in high regard throughout Iroquois history. On his passing, the leaders of the Confederacy gathered to pay tribute to a man who had fulfilled his duties with dignity, wisdom, and an unrelenting commitment to traditional beliefs.

DESKAHEH: AN IROQUOIS HERO

Throughout the long history of the Iroquois, there have been many women and men who have become heroes because of their courage, dedication, and compassion for their people. Traditional Iroquois place a high value on community service, humility, and generosity; they view with contempt those who devote their lives to the accumulation of material things at the expense of these ancestral values.

In the last hundred years, few Iroquois sacrificed as much for the people as Levi General, a Cayuga man who lived as a farmer on the Six Nations Grand River territory west of Hamilton, Ontario. General was a noted linguist among the people of the Grand, speaking not only his Native language but also the other five Iroquois dialects as well as English.

General was born in 1872 and labored for some time as a lumberjack before turning to the land. In time he was blessed with a supportive wife and nine children. Because of his natural patience, stable domestic life, and natural skills as a speaker, he was selected in 1917 to fill one of the positions on the traditional Cayuga council and given the ancient title of Deskaheh.

It was not a peaceful time to become a spiritual and political leader of the Iroquois of the Grand. World War I had been tearing Europe apart for three years. The weary Canadian army was demanding ever more young men to risk their lives on the blood-soaked battlegrounds of northern France.

Many of the soldiers were recruited from the various Iroquois communities, with a particularly large contingent coming from the Grand River territory. Those who survived the trenches returned to their reservation homes with new ideas as to how the affairs of the residents should be governed. With the active support of the Canadian government, they sought to replace the traditional Confederate council with a system rooted not in sovereignty but defined by a set of alien rules called the Indian Act.

Deskaheh was adamantly opposed to any attempt to undermine the authority of the Confederacy. His determination to preserve the treaty rights of the Iroquois compelled him to seek the intervention of the highest British authorities. Accordingly, he traveled to England in 1921 to appeal directly to King George V, only to be denied an audience with the monarch.

His efforts drew considerable press attention, which in turn resulted in the Canadian government targeting him as a particularly troublesome man. He was harassed by the authorities, yet refused to be intimidated.

Like many leaders, Deskaheh took the actions of U.S. President Woodrow Wilson to heart when he created the League of Nations, in part to give a voice in international affairs to the smaller nations of the world.

After being forced to abandon his farm and chased out of Canada by the Royal Canadian Mounted Police, Deskaheh decided he would return to Europe to seek the intervention of the League. Using an Iroquois passport, he arrived in Geneva, Switzerland, in September of 1923, the home of the League of Nations. He spent over a year in Geneva preparing petitions, seeking meetings with foreign delegates, and speaking out about the injustices Canada had committed against their former Iroquois allies.

Isolated, impoverished, and largely ignored, Deskaheh persisted with his efforts to secure a hearing for the Iroquois,

Haudenosaunee Chief Leon Shenandoah "Tadodaho." Photo © Marcia Keegan

until the stress began to undermine his health. He left Geneva in January 1925, weakened and defeated.

The Cayuga chief tried to return to his family and farm, but was denied entry into Canada by an embarrassed and vengeful government. He was compelled to take refuge on the Tuscarora Reservation across the Niagara River from Ontario.

In his final speech, given in Rochester, New York, Deskaheh said: "The fathers among our people have been real men. They cry out now against the injustice of being treated as something else."

It is said he died of a broken heart on June 25, 1925, his face turned toward his beloved Grand River.

TADODAHO LEON SHENANDOAH: AN UNCOMPROMISING LEADER

Leon Shenandoah, the late Tadodaho of the Haudenosaunee Confederacy, commanded the respect of everyone he met, even those who actively sought his removal from power. Shenandoah was returned to the embrace of Mother Earth July 24, 1996, before the largest assembly of Iroquois in modern times. Many of those who went to Onondaga to pay homage to the Tadodaho were opponents of the Confederacy and had defied the principles he held sacred.

Gathered at the Onondaga longhouse were the traditional Haudenosaunee clanmothers, faithkeepers, and chiefs Shenandoah had worked with for most of his adult life. As the chairman of the Confederacy, he had also taken an active role in supporting legitimate leadership against those who placed the sovereign rights of the Iroquois at risk.

Shenandoah opposed the exploitation of the collective rights of the Iroquois for individual profit. He clearly saw the dangers in the development of an economic class system dominated by an elite few. He stood against gambling, tobacco smuggling, gun running, and so-called "warrior" societies. He made many statements condemning the greed that had taken over the minds of some Iroquois. He joined with the traditional Haudenosaunee when they boycotted outlaw businesses, set up roadblocks to exclude state officials from Iroquois territory, or banished those who refused to obey the laws of their nations.

Those engaged in illegal businesses brought violence to the Iroquois by forming heavily armed paramilitary organizations to protect their operations against the regulatory efforts of the Confederacy, New York State, or the U.S. federal government. Shenandoah repeatedly criticized their actions as being contradictory to the Great Law of Peace, which is, in effect, the Iroquois constitution.

One of the things that maddened his opponents was his refusal to consider the quick-buck schemes they said would enrich the Iroquois. Whether it was fireworks, gasoline, casinos, or alcohol, if Shenandoah thought an activity would violate the Great Law, he turned it down— even if it meant the traditional Iroquois would have to exist without some of the more distracting material things in modern society.

Many of those outlaws, gaming advocates, and wayward business owners went to Onondaga for Tadodaho's funeral services. Their presence was shocking to other Iroquois since some of them had made public statements calling for the execution of the Haudenosaunee chiefs, including Leon Shenandoah.

Shenandoah was no idle dreamer. He was a political realist who repeatedly cautioned Native leaders against exploiting their sovereignty for short-term gain. He believed such things as casino gaming is but the latest tactic by the U.S. government to undermine and ultimately destroy Native people.

Shenandoah had deep insights into the hearts and minds of American politicians because he was a student of history and a keen observer of people. Every political or economic action had its attendant effects, and Shenandoah knew careful thought had to be applied to the logical consequences of the Confederacy's actions before decisions were made.

By no means was Shenandoah passive or hesitant to speak his mind. He feared no one. He lived a materially simple life, which made any attempt to corrupt him futile. He was an old-fashioned, Iroquois-stubborn man who held his own during times of radical change. He knew the world would one day tire of this mad dash towards a material nirvana, but not before paying a heavy ecological price for its greed. He was fond of reciting the ancient prophecies supporting his view that the era of purification is now upon us.

As chairman of the Confederacy, Shenandoah enjoyed great prestige, but he was ever the truly humble man who took delight attending the traditional ceremonies. He moved slowly, deliberately, and was always ready to greet friends and guests with a gentle smile while tapping tobacco into his corncob pipe.

Leon Shenandoah was one of those Iroquois leaders who will be remembered with fondness many generations hence. He set a standard for behavior and dignity that we will be hard pressed to emulate. He accomplished miracles as Tadodaho and fulfilled his duties as a human being to his family, his nation, and to the Creator.

Perhaps this is why so many were drawn to his funeral, as if attracted by the divine light that guided Leon Shenandoah.

On The Passing of a Good-Minded One

On September 4, 1996, Bernard Parker, a Seneca Nation roti-iane (literally a good mind), died of complications arising

Seneca Nation Chief Bernie Parker, right, with Onondaga Nation Chief
Louis Farmer, left, at the 1994 Treaty of Canandaigua commemoration,
Canandaigua, New York. Photo © Joanne Shenandoah

from an infection of his pancreas. Mr. Parker did his family justice in all areas of his life. He was only sixty-one when he left us for the Creator's land, where he will be welcomed by those ancestors he had honored with his life's work

Chief Parker was by all accounts a remarkable man who set a very high standard for leadership among the Iroquois. He was born and raised on the Tonawanda Seneca community in western New York, the offspring of a remarkable family whose reputation for creativity had inspired the Haudenosaunee over many generations.

I had known Chief Parker for many years, first meeting him at a Grand Council session at Onondaga. He was a solid, athletic, handsome man, naturally attuned to the patience, diplomacy, and compassion his stature as a spokesman for the Seneca Nation required.

He never hesitated to become actively involved in the issues before the Confederacy; his advice was listened to with care, for he selected his words deliberately and with much forethought. He never spoke in anger yet there was never any doubt where he stood on matters that affected his family, clan, and nation.

Parker stood strong with the other Haudenosaunee leadership against the temptations of the day. He was well versed in his own nation's history and customs, with a firm command of the spiritual rituals that are essential to the survival of the Iroquois as distinct people.

Parker could not be moved from his stance against those activities that compromised the sovereignty of the Haudenosaunee. By saying no to various economic development plans he thought immoral, he incurred the wrath of a small group of Senecas, but he never wavered.

In conjunction with the Seneca Nation Council, he held that banishment of those who would disrupt the peaceful lives of the people was justifiable in some instances. For this stand he was attacked physically, while also having to weather assaults on his character. Parker held firm.

He had the respect and love of those who knew him best. He responded to every call for aid from other Iroquois nations. As Mohawks we knew we could rely upon his common sense during times of crisis, and we did so, many times.

Chief Parker was also a key member of the Confederacy's task force on taxation. Like all the Iroquois delegates, he agreed it was important to provide for the material needs of our people, but the current situation meant we had to proceed in this direction with utmost caution.

Parker enjoyed good health for most of his six decades and was an excellent athlete in his younger years. He played lacrosse and was elected to the Western New York Softball Hall of Fame.

Like thousands of other Iroquois, he served in the U.S. Army. He returned home to work as an electrician to support his wife Maxine and their three daughters and two sons. He was pleased to be seven times a grandfather, and he served as a role model and mentor to countless others.

Rotiiane Bernie Parker Ga-na-gi-to-we has moved on to be embraced by the universe. We on this earth grieve at his passing, but are comforted by having known a truly great leader, one whose example shall stand for generations to come.

IX

ONE PEOPLE, ONE EARTH

IROQUOIS LANDS

Prior to European colonization, the Iroquois exercised active dominion over most of what is now New York State. Of the 49,576 square miles of the state, the Iroquois held title to about four-fifths of the total area (approximately 39,000 square miles).

Traditional Iroquois boundary lines were quite specific as to which lands belonged to a particular nation. The Mohawks' territory extended from the Delaware River north to the St. Lawrence and included almost all of the Adirondack Mountains. Their boundaries to the east were Lake Champlain, Lake George, and the Hudson River. By adding up the area of the current counties within this region, the Mohawk Nation can lay claim to 15,534 square miles (or 9,941,760 acres) as having been alienated from their possession through various means, including fraudulent "treaties."

Oneidas recognized the West Canada Creek, the Unadilla River, and the foothills of the Adirondack Mountains in present St. Lawrence County as their eastern border with the Mohawks. They also knew their lands went as far north as the St. Lawrence River and south to below the Susquehanna. Using the same formula of equating county areas to indigenous Oneida territory, a figure of 5,819 square miles is arrived at (or 3,724,160 acres).

Aboriginal Iroquois territory was by no means restricted to current state boundaries. Mohawk lands extended into southern Quebec and eastern Ontario, while the Onondaga, Oneida, Cayuga, and Seneca territories stretched southwards into Pennsylvania. The Tuscaroras held a large region in North and South Carolina as a homeland; it was never ceded by treaty. While most of the Tuscaroras removed to New York in the early 1700s, many others elected to remain in the South.

To the west of the Oneidas were the Onondagas; their border followed the Tioughnioga River, Otselic River, and Chittenango Creek as it flowed into Oneida Lake. Within their original national boundaries are the counties of Jefferson, Oswego, Onondaga, Cortland, part of Tioga, and about half of Broome. Their total area was 2,670,720 acres or 4,173 square miles.

Cayuga lands between Rochester and Syracuse included Cayuga, Seneca, Chemung, Schuyler, Wayne, Tompkins, and part of Tioga counties. Their region was 3,123 square miles or 1,998,720 acres.

In what is now western New York, the Seneca Nation enjoyed fertile lakeshore fields and rolling terrain that was rich in wildlife. Their lands stretched from east of the Genesee River to the Niagara Peninsula and southwest to Lake Erie. An estimated 10,248 square miles (6,558,720 acres) were held by the Senecas until various land companies removed them to three small reservations in the early nineteenth century. The construction of the Kinzua Dam in the early 1960s cost the Allegany Senecas hundreds of acres of land that were covered by the newly created lake, as well as their few remaining acres in northern Pennsylvania.

Altogether the Iroquois Confederacy held as its own 24,894,080 acres of some of the most beautiful and resource-wealthy lands in all of North America. It is clear that traditional Iroquois were careful custodians of the earth, for nowhere in this broad expanse of territory was there a single polluted stream, hazardous waste site, or open landfill.

The Iroquois now hold but a fraction of their former lands. After years of expropriation by New York State officials, various public works agencies, and the United States, the following is what is left:

Mohawk land in New York has been reduced to 14,640 acres in Franklin County, referred to as the "St. Regis Indian Reservation" or, more correctly, the Akwesasne Mohawk Territory.

Technically, the Oneidas live on 32 acres in Madison County but have been purchasing additional lands. They now have an estimated 3,000 acres in their possession.

Only 7,300 acres remain to the Onondagas on their territory, mistakenly called a "reservation," south of Syracuse.

Cayugas have no land left in New York; they live primarily on the Cattaraugus Seneca lands or on the Six Nations Reserve west of Hamilton, Ontario.

Since the Senecas divided in 1848, the New York Senecas have dwelt in three New York counties. Tonawanda is the traditional capital of the Seneca Nation; and the Seneca are in possession of 7,317 acres in Niagara, Genesee, and Erie counties. The Senecas were required to buy back their ancestral land from speculators in 1850, when the United States refused to recognize their claims to protection under the 1794 Treaty of Canandaigua.

Just west of Tonawanda live the Tuscaroras, on 5,778 acres. They were initially granted the right to settle in Oneida territory, but were forced to move to Niagara County after the American Revolution.

Distinct from the Iroquois Confederacy, the Seneca Nation of Indians (not affiliated with the Seneca Nation at Tonawanda) is governed under a constitution on the U.S.

model. It controls the reservations of Cattaraugus (17,025 acres) in Erie County and Allegany (30,984 acres) in Cattaraugus County. There is in addition the small 640-acre Oil Springs Reservation northeast of Allegany.

Total landholdings of the Iroquois are about 86,716 acres remaining from the original 25 million, equivalent to 0.34 percent—or one third of one percent—of what we once had.

LAND CLAIMS

Finding a way to provide for a growing family is a difficult challenge for most people and was proving to be particularly hard for this young couple with two children.

They had worked hard over the years to put aside materials for the building of their home, which was by any standards quite modest. By trading work with a few other families, the couple was able to raise a log home and a small barn for livestock. They were farmers during a time when land values were low and labor costs very high—factors that compelled them to barter their skills and goods rather than spend what precious little cash they had carefully set aside.

Their acreage consisted of some bottomland and a mixed forest that provided them with wood for heat. They grew most of their own food, including corn, beans, and wheat. The land they had purchased also contained several acres of fruit trees, which they kept trimmed and free from infestation by insects.

When harvest time came, their hard work resulted in an excellent harvest, which they sold at a good profit. With the proceeds they invested in cattle and hogs. Additional money was spent on purchasing the latest tools and machines, which, they hoped, would cut down on the amount of physical labor they had to perform.

While their income was stable, at least for the coming year, social conditions were not. They were concerned about the education their children would receive when they were old enough to be sent off to school. Familial values seemed to be under attack from all sides. There was a possible conflict brewing with the fundamentalist Christian sects that had recently moved into the area, with some preaching a literal interpretation of the Bible and others favoring collective, communal living with no private property holdings. Their government was split into many factions that were the subject of widespread rumors about corruption at the highest levels. Any demand for an accounting of expenditures of public funds was met with silent hostility.

The couple were also alarmed when they learned that their political leaders were involved with land claims negotiations and that their current holdings—land they had sweated over for so long—might be given to others as part of a deal they could not seemingly control.

Many times the wife and her husband had attended public hearings. At these sessions they both raised objections to any territorial cession without greater popular participation; they had also lobbied for public hearings and universal approval of all final deals.

Although there was widespread agreement with the couple's position, the politicians insisted that the land negotiations be kept confidential, hidden from public scrutiny. The couple were branded troublemakers. When the land deal was announced, it came as no surprise to anyone that their farm was among those to be surrendered.

Devastated by their loss, the couple made the painful decision to leave their farm in central New York and emigrate west. As they made preparations to sell what they could, there was time to reflect on governmental policies that could so easily divorce a family from the land and destroy many years' work with the stroke of a pen.

Generations would pass before the bitterness of the loss of people's homes and lands would fade. The social upheaval caused by these forcible dispossessions would express itself in increased substance abuse, intra-family violence, loss of traditional teachings, and an almost complete obliteration of communal history.

This fictional couple could have been any of thousands of Oneida-Onondaga-Mohawk-Cayuga-Seneca Iroquois families between the years 1794 and 1830, when New York State engaged in a series of fraudulent land sales with corrupt Native leaders.

These so-called "treaties" not only made Iroquois territory available to European settlers, they also enabled New York to settle its outstanding Revolutionary War debts while making a handsome profit. Land speculation was a source of great corruption during those years, and some of the most prestigious "blue bloods" of the state were deeply involved. People with names such as Morris, Ogden, Phelps, Schuyler, Jay, and Knox literally stole the land from under the Iroquois in open defiance of U.S. federal law.

Their lust for profits almost destroyed the Iroquois and harnessed the current generation of New Yorkers with an enormous debt, one the present leaders in Albany have largely ignored. The fact is, almost all lands in this region belong exclusively to the Iroquois, having never been ceded according to law. But the Iroquois realize how painful it can be for a family to lose its home because of shady dealings by politicians now safely resting in their elaborate tombs along the Hudson.

Accommodations have to be made to expand the territory now comprising the various Iroquois reservations in New

York. A considerable amount of public money will have to be spent for the damages caused to the Iroquois when they were removed from their lands. A new political relationship will have to be forged with the Iroquois by a governor who will address the land claims issue before the electorate.

Past governors have avoided the land claims issue and used the tactic of dividing the Iroquois into factions. Iroquois leaders sense the bitterness building up within their societies as New York fuels the flames of internal dissent by forging alliances with ethnic Iroquois rather than with the Grand Council of the Iroquois Confederacy. The refusal to negotiate directly with the Confederacy on land claims prevents settlement of this issue.

In the end, however, it is the individual taxpayer and landholder who suffer. However sympathetic to the Iroquois, they have no choice but to fight for their homes, a confrontation the Iroquois seek to avoid and no one is taking steps to prevent.

What is clear is the need for greater public participation in the land claims process, with the people of the state insisting U.S. District Court Justice Neal McCurn lift his ban on the claims negotiations. This gag order has prevented the Cayugas, Mohawks, and Oneidas (all current land claim litigants) from enlightening the public as to the merits of their case. The gag order was to remain in effect as long as negotiations were taking place. Hearings need to take place in the small towns and communities directly affected by the claims. People have an absolute right to be informed about the claims, since everyone will be affected.

As for the Iroquois, there is no absolute right to claim territory for purely monetary purposes. Our Creator gave us our aboriginal lands in trust with very specific rules regarding its use. We are caretakers of our Mother Earth, not lords of the land. Our claims are valid only so far as we dwell in peace and harmony upon her.

Any other activity is prohibited under traditional Iroquois law; breaching the law negates our caretaker rights to Mother Earth and her resources.

MOHAWKS WILLL NOT SELL MOTHER EARTH

Given the deep political divisions at Akwesasne, trying to forge a united front on any issue has never been easy. In 1989, however, the Mohawks of Akwesasne put aside longstanding internal differences to submit a proposal to resolve the Mohawk land claims issue in northern New York. In April, representatives from the Mohawk Nation Council of Chiefs, Mohawk Council of Akwesasne, and St. Regis Tribal Council gathered in Albany to meet with New York State negotiators. The Mohawks had devoted considerable resources to an in-depth study of the land claims region, including the retention of an appraisal company to determine the market value of the disputed territory.

Akwesasne was, and currently remains, perhaps the most arbitrarily divided community on earth, with three internal Mohawk governments. The Mohawk Nation Council is the traditional government and part of the Haudenosaunee Confederacy. The St. Regis Tribal Council is a New York State agency restricted to the "American" side of the reservation, while the Mohawk Council of Akwesasne, on the Canadian portion, is empowered to govern by virtue of a Canadian statute called the Indian Act.

There have been instances of deep hostilities among the Mohawk councils, but in the 1980s there was movement toward consolidation of communal services such as health, justice, and education for the common good.

The land claims were also close to being resolved, but at the same time, internal divisions at Akwesasne caused by the rise of commercial gambling and tobacco smuggling were growing. State officials were aware of these conflicts.

In the summer of 1988, the Mohawks drafted a settlement proposal that was submitted to federal and state authorities in 1989. It is felt that state authorities, who in any case have shown little willingness to deal with land claims, purposely delayed responding when they saw that the Native united front was weakening. The coalition collapsed completely in the winter of 1989–1990.

Still, the Mohawks have not given up on the idea of a settlement even as they watch as the St. Regis Tribal Council, enveloped in the tentacles of gambling, contaminates its own people and devastates the precious few acres the Mohawks have left.

In 1999, the St. Regis Tribal Council was successful in opening a casino, an action that caused many Mohawks to suspect New York officials were working with the Council to secure a land claims settlement favorable to the state. These suspicions were heightened when the Mohawks learned in February 2000 that the Oneida Nation of New York was willing to exchange ten thousand acres of its claim area for slot machine options and the right to sell alcohol in its Turning Stone Casino.

The 1988 Mohawk proposal would have compelled New York to recognize that the state had violated U.S. federal law when it expropriated much of the Akwesasne reservation as defined by the 1794 Six Nations Treaty

The Mohawks' proposal asked for the return of St. Lawrence River islands along with a percentage of the profits from the public utilities that are using one of the islands to generate massive amounts of electricity. The Mohawks sought an annual rental fee of $32,768,795 from the Power Authority of the state of New York for the use of the St. Lawrence Power Dam, an amount that would have had a minimal impact on the finances of the state.

In addition, the Mohawks estimated the value of their mainland claim as $413.4 million of which a fair rental value would have been, in 1988, $37.4 million. The Mohawks also sought an exchange of the eleven thousand acres lost to New York for ten thousand acres of land in the Brasher State Forest, along with recognition of full Native jurisdiction over all territory returned to its possession. Funds would be set aside by the federal government to compensate the area counties for any lost revenues arising out of a claims settlement with the Mohawks, who would retain the right to purchase, at fair market value, property to add to the existing reservation.

The settlement offer was fair and would have no doubt received popular support had the Cuomo administration done the honorable thing and signed the agreement. Instead, the Mohawks were met with a counteroffer they deemed so "insulting" as to compel them to abandon negotiations, precipitating a decade of anguish culminating in the current rise of anti-Native land claims in upstate New York.

Still, the Mohawks have not given up on the idea of a settlement. A growing population has placed increased demands upon already limited physical resources, making expansion of the Akwesasne land base essential. The traditional Mohawks fear the Tribal Council will make an effort to trade original ancestral lands for expanded gambling compacts with New York. The Tribal Council could also move to have the other two Mohawk governments removed as participants in the claims, which could result in vigorous opposition on the reservation.

CAYUGA LAND CLAIM CASE

The resolution of the Cayuga Nation's land claim against New York was not resolved when, on February 17, 2000, a jury awarded them $36.9 million in damages for the loss of 64 thousand acres of land in 1795 and 1807. New York had been held in violation of the 1790 Federal Non-Intercourse Act, when it alienated Native lands through a series of "treaties" that resulted in the loss of almost all of the aboriginal Iroquois territory.

While the other Iroquois nations managed to hold on to at least a few acres within their ancestral boundaries, the Cayugas lost all of their homeland, an estimated two million acres in central New York State.

By 1795, the Cayugas were reduced to a 64-thousand-acre reservation, on the north shore of Cayuga Lake, that now includes the city of Seneca Falls. The Cayuga Nation Council of Chiefs has maintained the sale of the reservation violated U.S. federal laws, an argument that was sustained by the U.S. federal courts.

Negotiations between state officials and the Cayugas to resolve the claim were held over a period of years without result. The Cayugas then elected to seek compensation by jury. The Cayugas were seeking land and monetary damages from New York; they argued the value of the lost reservation, with improvements such as roads and buildings, was well in excess of $300 million. New York State officials disputed this figure, holding the true worth was no more than $51 million.

In an effort to avoid ongoing litigation, New York offered to resolve the claim for $130 million, but with the stipulation the Cayugas would have to abandon all future land claims and would be restricted forever to ten thousand acres of land plus an additional three thousand acres to be designated as "forever wild." New York also wanted the Cayugas to agree to abide by a trade and commerce contract, which would regulate business activities on the Native lands, and to adhere to state environmental standards.

The Cayugas refused, holding firm on their position that they have legitimate title to their aboriginal territory and could not, by virtue of their own laws, cede land they consider sacred. Nor would they accept any state laws since they were citizens of their own nation with a formal treaty relationship with the United States.

The Cayuga decision to reject New York's final offer on the eve of the trial meant a $93 million reduction in funds that they were planning to use to purchase land and reconstruct a Native community in the Cayuga Lake region.

As significant as the monetary amounts were, the Cayugas stated repeatedly they would take land over money. This position was undermined when U.S. District Court Justice Neil McCurn ruled prior to the trial that land would not be included in any award.

Judge McCurn conducted the trial in Syracuse before a panel of nine juriors, all of whom were from central New York, an area that has witnessed the rise of an anti-Native movement over the past few years, stimulated in part by Iroquois land claims. While much of the United States has enjoyed economic prosperity over the past decade, most of New York has experienced fiscal stagnation due to high taxes and the flight of many industries from the Northeast to the South and West. Local residents have been concerned a resolution of the Native claims would impose a heavy financial burden on landowners who are already among the most heavily taxed in the United States. Also, the region's small businesses, such as gas stations and convenience stores, were upset with the tax-free status enjoyed by Native retailers.

One group in particular, the Upstate Citizens for Equality, has proven to be very effective in commanding the attention of the local and national media in its campaign to bring an end to Native status, including the elimination of all Iroquois reservations. They have also initiated legal action to void the Oneida–New York State gambling compact through which the Oneida Nation of New York was able to open the Turning Stone Casino in 1993.

As of February 2000, UCE claimed a membership of over 8,000 people mostly centered in the Cayuga and Oneida land claim areas. The organization grew rapidly after the Oneida Nation of New York decided to update its claims by naming thousands of homeowners in Madison and Oneida counties as defendants in its suit against New York.

The lawyers for the Cayuga Nation were concerned that the intense anti-land claim mood in central New York would subvert their client's right to a fair and impartial trial. They were denied a motion to remove the case to New York City and were also refused permission to call upon the Cayugas to testify as to the cultural, spiritual, and physical damages they had suffered as a result of territorial displacement. The Cayugas were also prohibited from calling upon historians to explain the circumstances of the claim, but instead had to rely on real estate appraisers to affix a dollar value on the disputed land.

New York countered with its own "expert," whose figures were accepted by the jury. The Cayugas were given $1.9 million for "rental" of the 64-thousand-acre reservation over the past 204 years and $35 million as the "current market value" of the land.

No decision was made as to who will actually pay the award. Before the trial, U.S. federal officials had offered to contribute half of the state's $130 million proposed settlement, which was withdrawn when the trial began.

The Cayuga Nation has its offices near the Cattaraugus Seneca Reservation south of Buffalo, New York, where an estimated 448 Cayugas reside. There are over 2,200 Seneca-

Cayugas in Oklahoma and hundreds more on the Grand River (Six Nations-Oshweken) Reserve in southern Ontario.

The Cayuga Nation promised an immediate appeal of the jury decision, referring to the award as "irrational." There were no immediate responses from the other Iroquois nations as to how the Cayuga decision would affect their claims.

IROQUOIS POPULATION

No one truly knows the exact number of Iroquois living in the United States and Canada. We do know our current population is far less than it was in 1492, when we had large towns and villages scattered over a region that stretched from present Quebec City to mid-Pennsylvania. At the time of European contact, there may have been upwards of 100,000 Iroquois. Physical evidence seems to sustain this argument, because there is virtually no place within our aboriginal territories that was not settled, cultivated, or otherwise occupied by the Iroquois.

European explorers, fur traders, and missionaries noted that our communities were fairly large, consisting of hundreds of people living in longhouses, sometimes over three-hundred feet in length. Around these towns were hundreds of acres of fields up to eight miles in length and planted in corn, beans, and squash, as well as large apple and peach orchards.

Along the St. Lawrence, the Mohawks had two very large towns called Hochelaga (Montreal) and Strathacona (Quebec City), which were visited by the French navigator Jacques Cartier in 1534. Cartier was impressed by the size of these places, which he estimated as containing many thousands of residents.

Anyone who has studied urban planning knows any large town or city does not exist in a vacuum, but requires an elaborate network of goods and services to survive. If Cartier was correct in his observations, these two towns would have been supported by many other Mohawks engaged in securing food, building homes, conducting trade with other nations, or providing administrative and public works services.

By taking into account the many dozens of other large Iroquois towns, the fertility of our lands, ready food supply, exceptional physical health, and stable social conditions, it is safe to state that the Haudenosaunee people were very numerous.

One of the rationales used to steal Indian lands was that America was little more than a "howling wilderness" barely inhabited by a people who were primitive savages. Such a lie cannot be sustained in light of recent research. In his book, *The Native Population of the Americas in 1492*, Professor William Denevan of the University of Wisconsin estimates that there were between 43 and 65 million Native people living in the Americas at the time of European contact, with as many as 4.5 million Indians in what are now the United States and Canada. There are now less than 2.5 million Native Americans residing in North America, according to the latest census figures.

Our fall from that pinnacle of prosperity was terrifyingly swift. Millions of our ancestors died in massive European-bred plagues prior to active colonization. Countless others died as a result of warfare or slavery. Within a decade of the landing of Cristobal Colon on Hispaniola, well over a half million Indians died on that island alone.

And so it went, as Native nation after nation was "discovered," attacked, forced into retreat, and finally restricted to marginal lands incapable of sustaining the lifestyles they had developed over many thousands of years.

Only during the past three generations have Indians begun to increase in numbers. The Iroquois, like other Native peoples, have slowly begun to recover from centuries of population stress. By the latter part of the twentieth century, the

Iroquois were experiencing a population surge as overall health conditions improved. According to the latest data, there are 74,518 Iroquois in North America, the majority of whom live in Canada.

The latest detailed figures for New York State list 16,754 Iroquois living on, or registered with, six reservations: Akwesasne, Oneida, Onondaga, Tonawanda, Tuscarora, Cattaraugus, and Allegany. Every Iroquois nation except the Cayugas has at least a small foothold in their original territories.

In New York State, the figures indicate Akwesasne has 5,632 Mohawks; Oneida has an enrollment of 1,109; there are 1,596 Onondagas; 1,200 Tuscaroras; 448 Cayugas (primarily living at Cattaraugus); 1,050 Senecas at Tonawanda; and 6,531 Senecas at Cattaraugus and Allegany.

In Quebec, the most recent figures indicate there are 1,753 Mohawks at Kanehsatake-Oka and 7,878 Mohawks at Kahnawake. Ontario has 7,766 Mohawks registered on the "Canadian" side of Akwesasne; 5,728 Mohawks at Tyendinaga; 557 Mohawks at Wahta-Gibson; and 3,970 Oneidas at Southwold near London, Ontario. There are 17,603 Iroquois of all Six Nations on the Grand River Reserve west of Hamilton.

In Wisconsin, 10,309 Oneidas live in the Green Bay area, while 2,200 Seneca-Cayugas are living on a small reservation in northeast Oklahoma.

In arriving at a total, consideration must be given to the estimated thousands of Iroquois who have lost their status through intermarriage or because they have not lived on a reservation for some time. At Akwesasne, the numbers are not indicative of the true population of the reservation since enrollment can be duplicated on both sides of the border. Also, some traditional Iroquois have refused to be counted in either the Canadian or U.S. census, which affects the final numbers.

X

AKWESASNE WHIRLWIND

MAY 1: AN HISTORIC DAY FOR THE MOHAWKS

May 1st has come to have great meaning to the Mohawk Nation. It was on this day that two events took place that have had great impact on the lives of the people of Akwesasne.

Over a hundred years ago, American and Canadian authorities enacted policies to undermine the traditional government of the Mohawk people and replace it with administrations that would serve the assimilationist plans of Ottawa and Albany. During this period, Americans spoke of the "vanishing redman," who was confidently expected to disappear, becoming merged in mainstream society. Every effort was made to achieve that result, to wipe out a distinct Native identity through education, territorial displacement, administrative maneuvers, divisive strategies, and outright extermination if the Indians dared to resist.

As part of this agenda, New York State, in 1892, in clear violation of U.S. federal law, set up the "elected" St. Regis Tribal Council as the "legitimate" Mohawk government in the American side of Mohawk territory.

The Mohawks and other Iroquois refer to such colonial agencies as the "elected systems" and have been vigorously fighting them ever since they were imposed upon the Native people.

The Canadian government has also tried to keep the Mohawks divided by imposing its "elected" system at Akwesasne. Since Akwesasne is split in half by the international border, Ottawa's agents were in a position to take a few lessons from their American counterparts and replace the longhouse chiefs with Ottawa's own lackeys.

At dawn on May 1, 1899, under cover of fog, a small contingent of Mounties entered Akwesasne to apprehend the chiefs. They had called the Mohawks to a meeting in the local council house, under the pretext of looking for workers for a bridge construction project.

When the chiefs entered the building, the Mounties moved to make them prisoners only to be met by John Fire-Saiewisakeron (also known as Jake Ice), a brother of one of the chiefs. In the ensuing scuffle, Fire was shot and killed by Lt. Colonel Sherwood, the officer in charge. The chiefs were taken to jail, where some of them remained imprisoned for over a year for no other reason than that they opposed the new "Indian Act" government.

Three generations later, on May 1, 1990, tragedy again struck the Mohawk people when two Indian men died at the end of a four-day battle said to have set off the most intense gunfire on Canadian soil since the Metis conflict (or Louis Riel Uprising) in the 1870s.

For two years prior to that day, the reservation had become the scene of unrestricted criminal enterprises ranging from tobacco smuggling to casino gaming. Controlling these activities was beyond the ability of any of the three Mohawk councils, which was understandable given their distrustful past relations. Compelled to action because of the growing anarchy and increasing violence, hundreds of Akwesasne residents erected barricades on either end of the reservation on March 23 of that year in an effort to end both smuggling and gambling.

The casino operators retained heavily armed gangs to break down the barricades. On April 24, the anti-gamblers were forced to flee the reservation after sustaining consider-able automatic gunfire.

A few Mohawks elected to remain, however, to defend their homes. One of these residences was that of my brother, and rather than leave him at the mercy of his opponents, I elected to stand with him. I would not have been much of a human being if I had deserted him at such a time.

We stayed at his home for four days, taking an increasing amount of gunfire. There were only a handful of men with us, but we held on. During the early morning hours of May 1, Mathew Pyke, 23, and Harold Edwards, 32, were shot. Pyke died some hours later in the Malone, New York, hospital, and Edwards never made it to the emergency room.

I, along with my brother and three others, were arrested and charged with the murder of Harold Edwards. We were all cleared during the preliminary hearing. The killings remain unsolved and a source of considerable tension at Akwesasne.

Given these past injustices, it is no wonder May 1 has come to have special meaning for the Mohawk people.

AKWESASNE:
THE WAR AGAINST THE EARTH MOTHER

Onen non:wa ehnon:we nentsitewate nikonhraie:ra te Iethi nistenha Ohontsia tsi ne e taiakohtka wenha:kie tsinaho:ton ionkionhehkwen. Iotshennon:niat tsi she:kon teionkihsniekie tsini:iot tsi shakohrienaien:ni ne shahakwata:ko ne tsiionhontsia:te.Ne ionkhihaw-ihshon ne onkwehshon:a tanon kario:ta:shon:a tsinikari:wes ohontsi:ke teionkwatawen:rie. Ne kati ehnon:we iorihwa:ke tsi entewatka:we ne kanonhwara-tonhtshera.

Ehto niiohtonha:k ne onkwa nikon:ra.

"We are thankful to our Mother, the Earth, for she gives us all that we need for life. She supports our feet as we walk about her. It gives us joy that she continues to care for us as she has from the beginning of time. To our Mother, we send greetings and thanks.

"Now our minds are one."

The light of an early winter morning comes filtered through the ice-encrusted windows of a plain rectangular building. The exterior of the 70-by-30 foot structure is painted an off-white; it is bordered by cedar trees that capture a cold breeze and send it down to the ground, where the snow dances in swirling circles.

Inside, two roaring woodstoves on opposite ends of the room cast off waves of heat across the wide floor. There are two tiers of benches braced against the four walls, a table laden with cups and bowls, and nothing more. A door stands at the eastern side of the building and another, directly opposite, to the west. Ten windows, single pane and shivering in the wind, are spaced high on the walls.

Gathered before the east stove is a small group of men and women sitting on benches. They are slowly emerging from their cocoons of heavy coats, gloves, and hats. One man, of medium height, with black hair, stocky build, and a face reddened by the cold, stands and faces the stove. He opens the fire door, clears his throat. From an ash splint basket he takes a pinch of green tobacco. He begins to speak, his words hypnotic, fluid, and strong. As he talks, he loses sight of the people, his eyes concentrating on the flames before him. The people are quiet, paying close attention to his words. The men bow their heads, their arms braced on their legs, heavy hands clasped before them. They sit with eyes closed, in deep meditation.

Among the Haudenosaunee, inheritors of the Great Law of Peace and citizens of the Iroquois Confederacy, there are no more important words than those spoken by the middle-aged man standing before the fire in the ceremonial longhouse in the center of the Mohawk territory of Akwesasne. The name Mohawk was hung around their necks by ancient enemies. It means "man eater" and refers back to a time when the ancestors of the people gathered around the fire had developed a taste for human flesh. But that was long ago. They refer to themselves as the Kaiienkehaka, the People of the Flint. They were the first people to accept the teaching of the prophet, a Huron (Wyandotte) man of virgin birth called the Peacemaker. He converted the Mohawks en masse and instilled deep in their hearts a sense of purpose in the world and the dream that one day all humanity will be united in a great League of peace and harmony.

The man in the longhouse recites a prayer of thanksgiving. He begins by expressing a collective greeting to the Mother Earth and the gratitude her children feel for the gifts of life. He will then address the waters, medicine plants, food crops, trees, insects, animals, birds, winds, thunder, moon, sun, stars, and spiritual beings. Finally, he will speak to the Creator, a "faceless" entity that is, according to the Iroquois, the totality of all that is and is most certainly conscious.

No ceremony, communal meeting, or social gathering can take place among the traditional Iroquois without the thanksgiving prayer. It brings the spirits and minds of the people together, extinguishes anger, and emphasizes the basic goodness and beauty of life. Through these words the Iroquois harmonize their lives with the natural world: as it goes with the Mother Earth so, too, it is with her children. And in Akwesasne, the blood-milk of the Mother has become lethal.

It is an American Indian community like no other on Turtle Island. Located sixty miles southwest of Montreal, it sits astride the St. Lawrence at the confluence of the Grasse, Racquette, and St. Regis Rivers. There are over thirty islands within its 28,000 acres but most of Akwesasne's 9,000-plus inhabitants reside on the mainland. Subdivided into sections claimed by New York, Ontario, and Quebec, it is patrolled by seven different police agencies and has three Native governments, two of which were forced upon the Mohawk people by the U.S. and Canadian governments. The third is the traditional Mohawk Nation Council of Chiefs, a member of the Iroquois Confederacy and the overseer of the many elaborate ceremonies that define aboriginal beliefs and practices here.

Given the artificial political and legal divisions on this mid-size reservation, it would be most surprising if consensus was reached on any issue. For the most part, there is no unity. The Canadian- and U.S.- backed governments continue to press for policies and plans that would gradually result in the total assimilation of the Mohawks into the North American cultural mainstream. Among their initiatives are commercial gaming and heavy industry, as well as turning parts of the reservation into an open landfill to receive the garbage from surrounding non-Native communities.

Opposed to them, but without any financial means, is the Mohawk Nation Council. For many years it has fought an intense battle to prevent Akwesasne from turning into a neon strip, but faces almost insurmountable odds in its efforts to sustain a way of life alien to modern mainstream culture.

Officials in the Bureau of Indian Affairs and the Department of Indian Affairs (its Canadian equivalent) deny the existence of the "Mohawk Nation." Such funds as are earmarked for Akwesasne go to the "elected" systems, leaving the Mohawk Nation to appeal to the spirit of the people, since it cannot deliver any services. As might well be suspected, the internal factions among the Mohawks are deep and sometimes deadly.

It was not always this way. The retreat into chaos began on April 25,1959. It was then that the United States and Canada joined to celebrate one of the most significant engineering accomplishments of the twentieth century: the building of the St. Lawrence Seaway. This massive project took but four and a half years to complete, but when it was done the mighty St. Lawrence had been changed from a fast-flowing, cleansing artery into the Great Lakes to a placid, almost dormant liquid highway for ocean freighters to carry cargo into the North American interior.

The St. Lawrence had been dug up, redirected, and dammed. Its waters were funneled through turbines to produce hydroelectricity. Where it had raced along sandy beaches and sung across the rapids, there was now the stillness of a lake beneath whose surface lay the ruins of a dozen small towns. An active river-culture marked by fishing scows, single-car ferries, and winter skating around miles of massive ice flows carved by Canadian Arctic winds died in the spring of 1959, to be replaced by great ships carrying the flags of Panama, Liberia, and Greece.

Back then, within the active memory of our times, a family could do well on the river. Like the life blood of a mother, it provided all one needed to survive. The rapids scoured the waters clean so that when the river finally slowed at Akwesasne, it was a shimmering clear green. The turbulence brought a rush of rich oxygen deep into the waters. Species of fish such as sturgeon, walleye, northern pike, trout, and salmon took to the rich river beds with excitement. When the ice surrendered in defiant, crashing roars to the warmth of spring, the fish began to run, spawning by the millions. A family working together, with gill nets and spear, could catch enough bullheads in two weeks to take care of their financial needs for a year.

Trucks would come to Akwesasne from distant cities to load up with fish. The harvest went on throughout the day and night. The gill nets, some three hundred feet in length, were checked in the morning and dusk, while nighttime brought dozens of boats onto the river, with gas lanterns on their bows and men with long spears poised to hook fish brought to the surface by the light.

Fish were not only a means of securing an income but were the main source of protein for the Mohawks. Every riverside home had a dock and large fishbox to hold the best fish. Satisfying hunger was as simple as walking down to the shore and selecting dinner from the box. Whatever was not eaten or sold was traded for garden vegetables, for tools, for work, or given as a gift. The remains of the fish-cleaning attracted thousands of seagulls and other birds to bicker and feast. Anything left over was used to fertilize the gardens that every family tilled.

Natural proteins and carbohydrates made for strong bodies. The Mohawks of two generations ago were inevitably strong and healthy. They were not wealthy in the material sense, but they had enough. They grew their own food and made almost all of their utensils. Without the fallback of government services, they had to rely upon each other exclusively. Homes were constructed by common effort. The Mohawks got by without money because they could trade for whatever they needed. It was on the whole a self-contained world—intimate, stable, comforting.

Mohawk was their mother tongue; it was a language of the earth. Some English or French was necessary if one left the reservation, but it was not until after World War II that the mother tongue came under attack. Increasing pressure by the outside government pushed the children into full-time schools, where the speaking of Mohawk was discouraged. By the sixth decade of this century, many parents elected not to pass on the Mohawk language at all, because they feared it would hamper the children's learning.

Great factories were built to take advantage of the cheap hydroelectric power and the large pool of unskilled workers in the region. Powerful, arrogant, flush with cash, companies such as Reynolds Aluminum, the Aluminum Company of America (ALCOA), Domtar, Courtaulds Textiles, and General Motors built new factories or expanded old ones on the St. Lawrence. Employing thousands of workers in upstate New York, they became virtual lords of the St. Lawrence Valley. Area residents were beginning to suspect there was a connection between these industries and the diminishing fish, dying trees, and sick livestock, but local governments were unwilling to raise the issue.

While the regional non-Native communities were not prepared to challenge the corporations, the residents of Akwesasne felt they had little choice but to question the environmental changes that were beginning to seriously disrupt the indigenous economy and culture. Fishbeds were being gradually choked off by heavy weeds that flourished because the water and ice could no longer scour the river bottoms. Discharges from the industrial plants discolored the St. Lawrence for miles, made the water distasteful and dangerous to drink, and the fish unfit to eat. Soon warnings were being issued by health workers not to drink from the rivers or use the water to wash clothing.

The Mohawks were being pulled from the land, divorced from the Earth Mother. The air, water, and land were closing in on them. The very elements they had come to know and love were now blind to the smoke of their tobacco fires and deaf to the prayers of a confused people.

Without a diet based on fish, Akwesasne underwent a radical change. More processed foods were being eaten, especially sugars, milk products, and wheat flour breads. With the loss of resource-based employment came a reliance upon social services such as welfare. An explosion in the population growth meant more people were living on a land base that could not expand.

The reservation's farmlands were chopped up into housing tracts, further reducing the community's ability to provide food for itself. The extensive wetlands and marshes on the eastern edge of Akwesasne were also being destroyed, resulting in a decline in waterfowl. Tillable acreage along the St. Lawrence was condemned and expropriated by the federal governments for use as dumping grounds for the hard clays dredged from the bottom of the St. Lawrence.

Many residents of Akwesasne were dairy farmers until it was discovered their cattle were dying because their teeth were rotting away. As more and more calves were born deformed and brittle boned, most of the farmers elected to sell off their herds. Reynolds Aluminum was sued by the Mohawks of Akwesasne in 1976 for fluoride contamination; the suit was settled out of court in 1984. The Mohawk farmers argued the deformities in their cattle did not show up until after the Reynolds plant was opened in 1959. Reynolds denied there was any connection.

The children of Akwesasne were being raised downwind from the industrial plants. They began to show evidence of environmental illness such as headaches, concentration problems, and bad teeth. The stench from the factories made the air hard to breathe, while the open discharges gave an oily taste to the river water. Children who had formerly spent most of their summer months rafting, swimming, or fishing were now warned to stay away from the river. They were divorced from the land and the waters, no longer able to speak to the Mother, her secrets hidden from them.

Thrust into a market, wage-earning, hard cash and credit economy, the Mohawks were at a competitive disadvantage. They became high steel workers in cities far from home or elected to continue their education in colleges across the country. With each level mastered in areas outside their communities, they became ever more divorced from their ancestral values, until it became almost impossible to communicate across the generations. Elders were removed from the homes because the new Mohawk nuclear family simply did not have the time or financial resources to care for them. As younger parents left the home for work, the tentacles of the mass media reached in to ensnare their children: television became the most important factor in the learning experiences of the post-sixties era.

This subtle war against the Mohawks' way of life was almost won by the mid-1980s. Without natural resources to exploit, Akwesasne turned to service jobs and then, in the wicked capitalistic spirit of the Reagan years, found new ways to make money. Using the rhetoric of Native sovereignty, these new Mohawk entrepreneurs pushed the federals away from the reservation and began their journey into the world of easy wealth. Why not use Native rights for profit? Why not take advantage of the white man's greed? Getting even can fatten bank accounts if done with energy and foresight.

By 1987 the Mohawks of Akwesasne had undergone an almost complete change from the fish-harvesting days of their parents. Unregulated casino gaming was bringing in millions of dollars a month, which, when added to the millions more made through the smuggling of cigarettes, drugs, and alcohol into Canada, made the reservation among the richest in North America. With this wealth came expensive electronic toys, automobiles, and homes, as well as the habits of consumer America—drugs, guns, and booze. Incidents of familial abuse were reported in alarming numbers, enough to warrant the building of a battered women's shelter. Significant communal resources were given to the staffing of two large social service agencies, while a call went out for psychologists to deal with attempted, and all too often successful, suicides.

Extensive studies were initiated to monitor environmental contamination. The results were shocking but not unexpected. Animals such as shrews, frogs, and turtles were examined in their natural habitat close to the factories. They were found to have been contaminated so heavily with known carcinogens as to require handling as hazardous wastes. Over the decade of the eighties, so many reports came from these studies that the children of the reservation could say polycholorinated biphenyls easier than "Kaniatarowaneneh" (the Mohawk name for the St. Lawrence). In addition, they knew what mercury and mirex did to human beings. They could see it in the eyes of their grandparents.

To combat the polluting of Mohawk territory, the Akwesasne Environmental Task force was created. Staffed by Iroquois, it has played a key role in securing U.S. Environmental Protection Agency recognition that at least part of Akwesasne is so heavily contaminated as to warrant listing as a Superfund cleanup site. The Task Force has pressured Reynolds Aluminum to admit it has in fact discharged PCBs into the St. Lawrence, and it has also sponsored a breastmilk study to monitor contaminants as they pass from mother to child. The Task Force has secured a place for Native people as key advisors on the St Lawrence River Remedial Action Plan and has created a mobile laboratory next to one of the most lethal dumpsites in North America. Information about the pollution at Akwesasne has been disseminated internationally, with the experiences of the community cited as one of the most blatant examples of the ecological war against the Mother Earth and her aboriginal guardians.

Virtually every conflict weathered by the people of Akwesasne over the past generation can be traced to the displacement of the people from their former way of life. Economic development alternatives to the marketing and exploitation of Native sovereignty through controversial activities such as gambling do exist; but without any firm internal cohesion, the implementation of a centralized business plan is highly unlikely. Without a common justice system, policing agency, or unified administrative entity, efforts to combat surface, air, and water contamination will continue to be sporadic, ill funded, and subject to political maneuvers beyond the control of those who truly have the well-being of the people and Mother Earth at heart.

In the longhouse, where the eastern light is cut off by a nearby two-story commercial bingo hall, the man before the fire completes the prayer of thanksgiving as the fire flickers to coals. His words affirm for a small number of Mohawks that life is a blessing, humans can dwell in harmony with Creation, and, if the faith is kept, the cycles of the seasons will continue to move as they have always done. At a time when the night seems to be without end and at its darkest, our children will, perhaps, live to see the coming of the new light in the east.

Ehto niiohtonha:k ne onkwa nikon:ra.

ANARCHY

Some say government has gotten too big and is stomping on the constitutional rights of the people. It's time, they argue, to get big government off the people's backs, give power back to the people, dismantle most federal programs.

This type of argument smacks of anarchy, which I know from personal experience is not a pretty thing.

In the spring of 1988, my home community of Akwesasne was on the brink of many wonderful things. Our Mohawk people were preparing to throw off the shackles of two hundred years of colonial rule and recreate our own Native courts, police service, educational system, and economy. Factionalized for over a hundred years by the imposition of government entities by the United States and Canada, many Mohawks nevertheless truly believe in one government, one people, one nation.

Our efforts were met with hostility by groups who were fearful of a single government and especially one that might prove to be popular, stable, and backed up by a strong justice system. Their arguments against a single indigenous governing body are often echoed by states' rights advocates, extreme right-wing Republicans, and self-styled militia groups across the United States, all of whom are opposed to Native independence.

A single Mohawk government would, our domestic opponents argued, interfere with business, frustrate individual initiative, stomp on the people's rights, and replace the work ethic with a welfare state.

Not content to challenge the drive for Mohawk unity politically, these "business" owners armed and financed a paramilitary protection outfit, which they insisted was created to protect the people against the intrusions of any external governing agency.

This paramilitary gang called itself the "Mohawk Sovereignty Security Force," and like their non-Native counterparts cloaked their true motives behind the flag of super-patriotism. In order to obtain the firepower they felt they needed to combat their opponents, they became part of an international arms network that stretches around the planet.

They succeeded in scaring off both Canadian and American police forces from Akwesasne and in intimidating the local leadership and preventing the enforcement of laws of any kind. Within this growing state of anarchy, an organized band of opportunists took charge.

Commercial gaming exploded at Akwesasne; within months of the retreat of responsible government, this small reservation along the St. Lawrence had become the third largest gambling center in the United States. Along with gaming, smuggling activities were greatly expanded to include not only cigarettes but alcohol, narcotics, and weapons. Tens of millions of dollars in illicit profits were made in an orgy of criminal activity. By the spring of 1990, it was the casino owners and smugglers who were dictating the social and political agenda for the Mohawk people.

No human society of any complexity can survive without organizing its collective concerns and delivering to the people the means to secure stability and survival. If any central government abandons its functions before either external or internal forces, other forms of control will be imposed by those who have the confidence to force their will upon the state.

Our Mohawk people were soon fighting their way out of the chaos brought about by the rise of a criminal class. Our experiences were in many ways similar to those of contemporary Russia, where people are now being pushed to extremes as they fight for their very survival as a nation.

But grand visions and high principles do not endure when they have been dragged through the mud of discord and organized hate. Our dreams for a united Mohawk Nation died in the spring of 1990, when we were in a state of civil war from which the wounds have yet to heal.

194 IROQUOIS CULTURE & COMMENTARY

During desperate times, people need the assurances a stable central government represents; we failed at Akwesasne to achieve this during the days of our greatest need.

Anarchy? We've been there and it's ugly.

SMUGGLERS CORRUPT MOHAWKS

The U.S.-Canadian border, which divides my home community of Akwesasne, presents an attractive and hugely profitable situation for smugglers of tobacco, alcohol, weapons, and illegal aliens—by both Akwesasne residents and opportunistic criminal elements from outside the community. By 1992, the Canadian government estimated it was losing over $300 million in revenues annually because of tobacco smuggling, most of which was occurring in Akwesasne.

Such great amounts of money were bound to attract criminal elements. The sound of gunfire became commonplace at Akwesasne, as smugglers defended their routes against any encroachment. Rumors continue to circulate about young men who have mysteriously disappeared while hauling cases of cigarettes across the St. Lawrence. According to local wisdom, when the sun goes down it is best to get off the river or risk being mistaken for a cigarette hijacker.

In 1998, U.S. Attorney Thomas Maroney of Syracuse brought criminal charges against twenty-one people for allegedly operating an international smuggling ring that transported $687 million worth of tobacco and alcohol through the Akwesasne Mohawk Territory from 1992 to 1996. According to the U.S. complaint, the smuggling web created by this group extended from California to Russia and so corrupted the St. Regis Tribal Council that the Federal government declared it to be a "criminal enterprise."

Among the defendants in the case were nine residents of Akwesasne, including the former head Chief of the St. Regis Tribal Council, the New York State-created and financed administrative agency. Also included were area residents Larry Miller, Nick Miller, Victoria Glines, Timothy Glines, all of Massena; Robert Browning of North Lawrence; and former New York State Trooper John Fountain of Malone.

The fact that most of the defendants were non-Native has not prevented a lawyer representing the Natives from claiming the alleged smuggling was lawful because it took place on sovereign Mohawk land and was therefore free from Canadian or U.S. jurisdiction.

The case quickly became obscured by claims of racial discrimination, aboriginal prerogatives, and treaty rights. For example, only nine of the defendants were Natives, yet the Tribal Council extended its claims of sovereign immunity to the non-Indians as well. This same council, which condemns the U.S. Justice Department as "racist," is the recipient of millions of dollars in Justice Department law-enforcement funds for its tribal police force.

It is important to note the ethnic Mohawks charged in this case were not members of the Mohawk Nation, nor do they have any connection with the Haudenosaunee Confederacy. In fact, this group was stripped of their Mohawk status a number of years ago, when they became involved in activities such as smuggling and gambling, which are contrary to the traditional laws and customs of the Mohawk Nation.

A convicted leader of the group, Loran Thompson, was at one time a member of the Mohawk Nation Council of Chiefs, but was removed from his position for his pro-gambling stance and his involvement in a physical assault in December of 1986 to which he later pled guilty in the Town of Bombay court. One of the other ethnic Mohawk defendants is former

St. Regis Tribal Council head chief Leo David Jacobs, an individual who was openly hostile to the traditional people throughout his term of office.

The Tribal Council he directed is an entity alien to the Mohawks, many of whom believe it was created to introduce New York State jurisdiction on Mohawk lands. The Mohawk Nation has repeatedly sought its removal from Akwesasne on the grounds that it lacks treaty status (and therefore sovereignty) and is not a part of the Confederacy.

A third defendant was Anthony Laughing, the former operator of the largest casino at Akwesasne. Mr. Laughing ignored the anti-gambling directives issued by the Mohawk Nation, claiming he was exercising his personal sovereignty by offering unregulated games of chance.

Since none of the defendants were citizens of the Mohawk Nation, or adhered to its rules, a defense citing treaties or aboriginal laws makes no logical (or legal) sense.

In the spring of 1988, the Mohawks were on the verge of a remarkable peaceful revolution. Officials of all three Mohawk governments at Akwesasne held a series of meetings to restore true sovereignty to the territory and agreed on the need for one peacekeeping service, one justice code, one education and health system, and one set of laws regarding trade and commerce.

The plan was to seek the gradual elimination of the international border that dissects Akwesasne, while bringing an end to the regulatory anarchy that stimulated smuggling. Some of those later convicted of smuggling organized successful resistance to the unity movement by taking part in the pro-gambling "warrior" activities of 1989–1990, the bitter legacy of a Mohawk community without the resources or will to control the flow of liquor and tobacco through its territory.

SMUGGLING ILLEGAL ALIENS

On October 5, 1998, two young women were arrested by federal officials in Montgomery County, New York, for allegedly smuggling illegal aliens into the United States. On December 10, another group of Mohawks was arrested for taking part in a smuggling ring that had made over $280 million in profits from the trafficking in human misery.

A primary alien smuggling route is across the St. Lawrence River, through the Akwesasne Mohawk Reservation, in a scenario such as this:

A high-speed boat spews white foam into the dark green waters of the St. Lawrence River as it flashes past boarded-up summer camps on the thirty-two islands that are a part of Mohawk territory. The driver flexes the throttle, increasing his speed as he crosses an open stretch of water. When he reaches the far side, he slows to search for a carefully hidden break in the deep marsh buffering the southern shore.

The boat is carrying human cargo this night, refugees from the economic crisis in southern Asia, desperate men and women, all young and terrified by the growl of the craft's twin Mercury engines and the brooding silence of the driver's armed companions.

Aliens, booze, dope, firearms—it's all the same to the smugglers. If they can make a buck by carting it across the river, consider it done. The risks are slight and the profits are more than tempting.

The boat driver is in command of the venture, his attention directed to the fast-approaching marshes as his partners adjust their portable scanners to catch any audio transmissions from the area police. They have, besides automatic rifles, night-vision binoculars, although these devices are almost useless as the fast-moving vessel bounces hard across the flow of the river.

The passengers are Asians—Chinese, Pakistanis, Vietnamese, Fillipinos—without exception driven by desperation to risk their lives and the limited resources of their families to make a stab at working in the United States, to find jobs that will provide for those left behind in rice paddies and urban slums.

They are no different in their grim determination than the Europeans of generations ago, those indentured servants sent across the turbulent Atlantic Ocean in leaking ships to a place of myth populated by heathens, radicals, slaves, and millionaires. Yet the apprehension about what lay ahead was eclipsed by the urgent need to escape a crowded, infested land, one which offered bitter fortune to those who sought to break free from the restrictions of class, religion, or ethnicity.

Then, as now, there are always the clever ones, ready to seize any opportunity to exploit the emigrants. The methods of finding their victims haven't changed much over the years. First, recruiting agents make their services known. Contact is made with the emigrant, whose family may have labored for years to save a partial payment for their journey across the Pacific.

The emigrants arrive in Canada using tourist visas. They are brought to the St. Lawrence River smuggling point in groups of ten. These particular Asians, huddled in the bottom of the speeding boat, are marked for the streets of New York City, where they will be pressed into sweatshops in conditions resembling slavery to work off the balance of their passage. Or the women may be forced into prostitution, to service clients along the East Coast. A few will enter the narcotics trade or turn their skills to exploiting other refugees.

Once the river boats touch shore, the human cargo is quickly transferred to large vans, either windowless or their glass made opaque with tinted film.

The van drivers, or "mules," are young kids eager to make $500 a head by racing the Asians four hundred miles through the backroads of the Adirondack Mountains before hitting the Thruway and entering Manhattan. With luck, they could be back the next day, having made more money in this one trip than their bewildered parents do in a month of arduous labor.

Without luck this time: flashing lights, handcuffs, and federal prison.

MY MOHAWK-ONEIDA FAMILY

MY HEROINE, MY GRANDMOTHER

Her maiden name was Josephine Susan Foote in English, but in her native Mohawk language her name was Kanenratirontha, or simply Wari:so:se (which is how the Mohawks say Josephine). She was born in the closing decades of the nineteenth century, when Native peoples were on the fringes of continental society, the supposed "vanishing Americans" doomed to extinction.

She spoke but limited English, enough to ask directions in unfamiliar places or buy food staples, but not much else. She was very shy and apt to disguise her bashfulness by drawing her shawl across her broad Indian face.

As the century turned, she met and married Jacob George, an Akwesasne Mohawk, tall and strong. George was a mason by trade, a man whose craft had been sufficiently developed to draw him away from the reservation to projects across northern New York and Ontario. He would be away from home for weeks at a time, and it was his wife who provided for the daily needs of a growing family.

They had nine children—six boys and three girls. All of them contributed to the survival of the family by working at tasks ranging from gathering wood to weaving ash splint baskets for sale on city streets.

Times were not easy. A Native family did not have welfare, food stamps, education benefits, or unemployment insurance. If they did not plant, hunt, or fish, they went hungry; if they did not work, they went ragged.

Wari:so:se would not have her children cry for food. She filleted fish, canned fruits, dried meat, and spent hours before a flickering kerosene lamp stitching clothes for her dark-eyed children. Most of the time she was content; her health was good and her family secure in having her at its center.

In her time the Catholic Church was omnipotent on the reservation. There were a few wayward Methodists, but the parish's Jesuit priest was the final word on birth, marriage, death, and politics. The daily masses provided Wari:so:se with spiritual comfort while weekly confessionals allowed her to share some of the problems that disturbed the rhythms of her family's labors.

There were, however, secrets that dwelt deep within the soul of Wari:so:se, things she sensed about herself that did not fit perfectly into the Catholic mold. She held all the Church's rituals to be absolutely sacred, without question or doubt. Yet at times she saw events in her dreams that a priest would be at a loss to explain, and was occasionally stirred by emotions she sensed ran deeper than the Faith.

The George family had over the generations given birth to "special ones," children who had the gift of insight and healing. Her husband's nephew Abraham was such a healer. It was said he was so powerful that he could cure serious illnesses by the simple laying on of hands. By the time he was a teenager, Abraham George was known far and wide as a miracle worker and a last resort when Western medical practices failed to relieve pain and suffering.

Wari:so:se also had the gift, although less developed than Abraham's. She saw events taking place in her dreams before they actually happened. She sensed the coming of visitors days before they actually arrived. She was rarely caught unprepared or by surprise. Her children were resigned to

Josephine Susan Foote George, "Kanenratirontha," at her home in St. Regis Village, Akwesasne, 1950. Photo © George family.

living with the "gift"—as small children they had learned to give up the useless practice of lying to their mother. She always sensed a misdeed or breech of the truth and was quick to trace a behavioral infraction to its source.

Wari:so:se was strict with her children but powerful in their defense. Most of them would grow up to leave the reservation, some never to return. Yet across the distances her love for her offspring never wavered, even when their actions caused her pain. She was patient and believed adversity could be waited out, the bad times would fade, and with a little luck she would have her family gathered around her once again.

This event would never happen, at least not in this world. Wari:so:se lost two of her daughters early on. One died of appendicitis, another during childbirth. Two of her sons left the area to find work, enlisted in the military during World War II, and afterwards drifted west. Another son settled on a nearby reserve, while her youngest daughter moved to Syracuse, leaving but three of her children to be with her as she entered her seventh decade.

It was in October of 1951 when Wari:so:se passed into the spirit world in a way that caused great sorrow to her family but was marked with dignity, self sacrifice, and honor. She left the reservation to help her daughter care for her newborn, a baby girl. As was her way, she was determined her granddaughter would be healthy and strong, as befitting one of her own.

At her daughter's second-floor apartment, located at the corner of West Genesee and Avery Streets, a fire broke out at 4 a.m., driving the residents into the street. Wari:so:se was told to leave, but when she could not find her grandchild she pulled away from her daughter to re-enter the apartment, now filled with smoke and the sounds of rapidly approaching fire.

Wari:so:se ignored the heat and flames and the risk to her own life. She brushed aside any feelings of fear and panic as she searched for the infant. When she found the small child, she carefully wrapped her in a heavy blanket to protect her from the fire. When she was satisfied the child was insulated, she carried the baby to the front door of the apartment only to find her way blocked by intense heat. She retreated to a window, searching for a way out, if not for her then for the baby.

By that time a small crowd had gathered around the building, waiting for the firemen to arrive. They saw Wari:so:se in the window and yelled for her to jump. The Mohawk grandmother knew she could not do so with the child. Instead, she paused, hoping someone would come close enough so she could toss the infant to safety. Finally, a man did come forward to catch the baby.

But who was strong enough to catch Wari:so:se? She hesitated to leap into the early morning, but the flames were quickly approaching; if she did not jump she would be burned to death. Wari:so:se stepped away from the building, into a warm space. She was killed instantly when her head struck a metal gas pipe protruding from the ground.

Having never known my grandmother, for she died four years before I was born, I nonetheless have always felt a deep and abiding admiration for her life and the circumstances of her passing. She was a self-defined woman, tough and compassionate. It is said no child ever left her home dirty or unfed. Her wishes were simple yet compelling: security of family, stability of home.

Through her the present generation lives on. As much as a grandchild longs to hear the voice and feel the touch of the strong hands of a grandmother, there is more than a little of Wari:so:se in our hearts and minds today.

THE BEST IN THE WORLD: ANGUS GEORGE

Some would say he was a great Mohawk—world-class athlete, fearless high steel worker, expert fisherman, master carpenter, and highly skilled craftsman with a rich command of his native language and strong opinions about the world.

To his mother Wari:so:se he was Sohahiio, the "Bright Road," but to his non-Native friends he was Angus "Shine" George, my uncle, the greatest lacrosse player of his time, a powerful man who in his prime carried 225 pounds of rock solid muscle on his six-foot frame.

His great strength came from years of labor in the lumber camps of the Adirondacks whose dark forested mountains absorbed a boy of twelve in desperate need of a job to provide for his younger brothers and sisters. It was 1922 when my uncle took up the axe and crosscut saw. Like many young people, he did not have the option of continuing his few years of schooling. His father, my grandfather, had drunk his way into obscurity, selling the family home for a few dollars and a bottle of whiskey.

Angus and his mother had come home from a long trek to town, where they sold splint baskets by the dozen, only to find out their house had been sold. They spent a precious few dollars on a small frame house across the road from their former home and there Angus labored with Wari:so:se to care for John-Katsitsiakeron, Peter-Ranikonhionni, Joseph-Tiawekate, Margaret-Kawennaronnion, Dave-Totkennion, and Ann-Konwationni.

Their possessions were few, but they ate well with fish from the St. Lawrence River, vegetables from the garden, and deer Angus shot with his .22 caliber rifle. No one went hungry among the Mohawks in those tough times; a family in need would have sacks of potatoes and smoked strugeon on their doorstep, placed there silently by neighbors.

During the winter months at the lumber camp, Angus carried water and wielded his axe while his mother wove sweetgrass baskets or tended to the children. When the snows melted they returned to the reservation to take part in the fish harvest, plant crops, and send the younger ones off to school for a few weeks.

Like all other Mohawk youths, Angus carried a lacrosse stick in his spare moments, twisting the hickory in his large hands, tightening the thick leather strings that formed a deep pocketed net for him to cradle a hard rubber ball. He realized he might have talent at the game when he took part in throwing contests at the local fair. As a teenager he hurled the ball with his stick farther than anyone else.

His solid build and firm stance adopted from months of heavy axe work made it impossible to push him aside. He used his heavy shoulder muscles to brush opponents out of his way; his muscles also gave him the power to hurl the ball at a target with bullet-like speed.

Lacrosse was a passion in Canada during the first decades of the twentieth century, with Native players ranking as the best in the world. From its beginnings among the Iroquois hundreds of years ago, it had become Canada's official national game. By the 1930s, it was tailored to fit in hockey arenas as a way of keeping the buildings full during the summer months.

The Iroquois were quick to adapt to the speed and finesse of box lacrosse, and Angus quickly became a star player. He had offers to play professional football and hockey but chose to stay with lacrosse. Given a contract to play in Vancouver at 21 years of age, he boarded a train in Cornwall, Ontario, for the week-long journey across Canada to the West Coast.

The money was good. There was enough for him to live well in British Columbia as a member of the North Shore Indians team and send funds home to care for the family. He enjoyed the acclaim as an athletic star and was honored to represent

Angus George "Sohahiio" at his home on the St. Lawrence River, St. Regis Village, Akwesasne Mohawk Territory. Photo © Native North American Traveling College.

Canada's Native people at the Los Angeles Olympics in 1932, despite having his game demoted to exhibition status.

Angus might have stayed in California, taking on Native roles in the movies; he had offers but autumn was coming and he longed to return home, to the rivers and forests where he would be with his family, weaving ash splint baskets and telling enchanting stories in their warm cabins beneath the heavy snows.

Angus played the game for three decades, and then hung up his stick to devote his time to fishing, working in his woodshop, and keeping a close eye on his beloved St. Lawrence. He thought and dreamed in Mohawk, reaching out to his mother and distant brothers who had left the reservation after World War II never to return. He did not care for the new ways and spoke bluntly, critically, of the latest generation of Mohawks, who had lost language and knowledge when they were forced from the woods and waters in the development craze of the 1950s.

Taken to a sterile hospital after becoming ill in his eighty-second year, Angus told his niece he feared losing his independence and wanted to go home. On January 8, 1992, Sohahiio was welcomed into the spirit world by Wari:so:se knowing he had done the best he could as a Mohawk and as a human being.

MY FATHER ENDURES
David George, Sr.-Tatkennion, 1925-1994

Our parents are more than providers, mentors, custodians, or teachers. They live within us, forming our physical, mental, and spiritual selves in such subtle ways we are often caught by surprise when someone comments we are behaving exactly like our mother or father.

We take comfort in the care and love provided by our parents and hunger for their approval though we must confront their flawed humanity and challenge their authority. Peace within ourselves comes only when we reconcile our individuality with our paternal and maternal creators. At the moment of their parting from this reality, we are entrusted with the responsibility of sustaining the shadow of their existence through our own finite biology. This is a good and necessary thing.

When my father passed into the spirit world at 2:30 a.m. on Wednesday, December 7, 1994, I thought his entry into another reality would produce a type of psychic shock wave all his children would feel. The strange thing was while I was not aware of his leaving until some hours had passed, my wife did hear knocking sounds at that time for which there was no physical explanation.

David George, "Tatkennion," Third Canadian Army, Brussels, Belgium, 1945. Photo © George family.

My father was a remarkably strong man. He was a mason for five decades, a craft learned from his father and passed on by his grandfather. He was praised by many for his creative skill with stone and mortar, a skill that supports many hundreds of homes throughout northern New York and eastern Ontario. As was his wish, he worked until the day of his death, never having to worry about losing his ability to use his powerful hands to sickness or infirmity.

When my brothers saw him in the emergency room, he was already dead and his body and face were surprisingly relaxed, as if the heart attack that killed him was little more than a discomforting spasm. He had a calmness marked by a hint of a smile. If we are to believe the ancient Mohawk traditions, at the moment he died he was welcomed into the spirit world by those he loved most in this life but had crossed over before him. No doubt, for him, he was embraced by his mother, a woman he could not talk about but with sad, lonesome emotions.

David George, Sr. was called Tatkennion (pronounced Dat-gen-yon) by his parents, the late Jacob George and Josephine Susan Foote George. His name means "he competes" in English, his second language. He was born and raised at Akwesasne although his life experiences would take him far beyond the reservation.

As a child of the Depression, he experienced deprivation of material things, but never doubted the care and affection of his family. Since he was a very handsome and strong young man, his mother was ever watchful as to the ladies who had designs on her baby boy. Only when he left her home to work during World War II in Syracuse was her grip relaxed enough for him to meet and marry my mother, who had heard so much about the formidable Mrs. George she would not leave the car when he finally brought her home.

It was while in Syracuse that he enlisted in the U.S. Army. He was sent to Kentucky for basic training, but when the Army found out he was technically a Canadian citizen, he was sent to Windsor, Ontario, and became a member of the Glengarry Highlanders. Not knowing he had already been to boot camp, his Canadian officers were greatly impressed by his quick grasp of infantry techniques. A smart man, that private George.

During the war he had many fascinating adventures. He met a short, pale, and rotund man while assigned in London to clean the debris caused by the Nazi V-2 missiles. The man called him "laddie," was polite and took time to find out who he was. He then learned this pleasant man was Winston Churchill, the British Prime Minister.

Later, in North Africa, he was on a plane that crashed into the desert. His platoon emerged from the wreckage bleeding, banged up, and in shock. Nonetheless, they were told to line up and stand rigidly at attention because Field Marshall Bernard Montgomery, the Allied Commander in North Africa, wished to review the Canadian troops. My father was not impressed, but he did shake hands with the man.

He would survive that experience to serve as a front-line fighter in Sicily, Yugoslavia, France, Belgium, the Netherlands, and Germany. He used to say the Germans were excellent soldiers but he was slightly better. He was an extremely accurate shot with a British Enfield .303 rifle, an ability that served him well when he was assigned to sniper-clearing duty by his company.

My father was part of the Allied occupying forces after the war. He visited the death camps in the area near Bremenhaven on the North Sea. I had assumed the Germans had such facilities only in Poland and the East. Not until I was at the U.S. National Holocaust Museum in Washington, D.C. did I learn there were many dozens of these killing places scattered throughout the Third Reich.

Upon his discharge, my father returned home, speaking better German than Mohawk for a time. He returned to Syracuse to work as a truckdriver before heading north and assuming his father's craft. His family grew rapidly, with fourteen children born by 1964. Two died in infancy. His wife, my mother, was an Avery from the Jefferson Street area and later of the Brighton district of Syracuse.

She was the keeper of the home while he worked long and hard at jobs on the reservation and as far away as Rochester. When she died of cancer in 1965, he was completely devastated and unable to adequately care for twelve children ranging in age from ten months to sixteen years.

None of his children deny he had serious problems with alcohol after the trauma of my mother's death and the breakup of his family. He spent many years inside the bottle, preferring its obliteration to the pains of consciousness. His life was prolonged because he was a fanatic about hard labor. Any lesser man would have been consumed by his lifestyle, as many were.

His pain was relieved when he met Barbara, who would become his second wife. They had four healthy children and a stable marriage. He hand-built another home, watched his kids grow up, and enjoyed his status as the patriarch of a family that included twenty-one grandchildren and two great-grandchildren.

Yet he never did escape his alcoholism, which in the end contributed to his death. His children refused to criticize or condemn him for this disease. When it came time for them to gather at his funeral, they did so willingly. This man was due respect, and he received it both by the integrity of the services and the large number of people who came to his wake.

Personally, I was always glad whenever I did something that pleased him. He stood by me during my time of troubles and would never hesitate to boast of my work. He was always supportive even if he thought I should do things differently. He was impressed by my selection of a mate, and my wife was glad to see the welcome in his eyes. He always had a keen eye for beauty.

I did not have the opportunity to listen to him very often during his last few years, but I am gratified to see the echoes of his face in the mirror, the movement of my hands, or the accent of my voice. It is my responsibility to keep his life stories intact, so those grandchildren who could not know him as a man will know of him as a remarkable human being whose contributions shall not easily fade from memory.

MIRACLE MAN RAY FADDEN-TEHANETORENS
Mohawk Historian, Iroquois Revolutionary

Revolutions are usually characterized by violent upheavals as the new order replaces the old. Political institutions are destroyed, opponents liquidated, societies collapse. Almost inevitably the fires of revolution consume those who spark it as the new leaders strive for stability by eliminating opponents, both real and potential.

All too often the new order, insecure and suspicious, suppresses the media and imprisons intellectuals. Emergency decrees are issued, civil liberties suspended, and the new police released to make their predawn arrests, filling the prisons and emptying the streets. Churches are closed while teachers are directed to instruct their students in the latest doctrines as the nation is recreated to fit the image of those who hold the reigns of power.

Not all revolutions are characterized by these developments, however. Contrary to the experiences of the Russians, Chinese, French, Iranians, and Germans, the Americans did not create a police state, but entrenched the political rights of upper class white males at the expense of all others.

In Iroquois country, there have been radical changes in our communities that can be called truly revolutionary. We first had the formation of the Confederacy, followed centuries later by accommodations to the Europeans, the great sufferings during the American rebellion against Britain, and the cultural rejuvenation as taught by the Seneca prophet Handsome Lake.

In time, however, the grind of reservation life took its toll on the Iroquois and particularly the Mohawks. Long accustomed to living free and unencumbered to travel as they wished, the Mohawks took to the new restrictions with anger and slow-burning resentment. Factionalized by arbitrary political boundaries, they saw their indigenous political systems suppressed, and their ancestral religious practices outlawed. By the twentieth century, the Mohawks had come perilously close to losing their identity.

We needed a teacher to remind us of our glorious past, of something positive and powerful we could take to heart as we prepared for yet another assault upon our traditions. As luck would have it, we had Ray Fadden, a teacher every bit as important to our history as Lenin is to the Russians, Mao Tsetung to the Chinese, and Benito Juarez to the Mexicans.

From his family home in the Adirondacks, this Mohawk man came to Akwesasne to challenge what our children were learning in schools and how they were being taught. He refused to go along with the standard texts. Ray had a remarkable way of stimulating his students to look within their own families to find the truth of their past. He believed by challenging the popular myths about Indians, which had depicted us as little more than savages groveling in the dirt, he would give us the intellectual tools to take on the world.

For Ray Fadden the children always came first. He had no tolerance for professional politicians, no desire to hold the reigns of power. He knew instinctively the great changes of any era began when the younger people had the courage to challenge the established order by demanding answers to their questions and resolutions of their concerns.

During a time when conformity was stressed in and out of schools, Ray was a maverick. He organized the Akwesasne Mohawk Counselors Organization, a group that traveled far and wide to collect information about Mohawk history and to visit the many sites where significant events occurred.

Left to right: Christine Fadden, Doug George-Kanentiio, Ray Fadden, "Tehanetorens," and Joanne Shenandoah, New York State Museum, Albany, New York, 1995. Photo © Joanne Shenandoah.

By exposing the students to historical geography, he gave them a sense of belonging to the land. His students made maps of Native North America, compiled lists of Indian contributions to the world, were involved in the making of traditional Iroquois clothing, and learned to conduct themselves as true human beings while in the forests or on the rivers.

Ray gave his students the priceless gifts of personal confidence, cultural security, and love for their unique heritage. His students would leave his classes excited by what they had learned. Many of them would turn out to be leaders of great merit, people such as Mohawk Nation leaders Jake Swamp, Ernest Benedict, Tom Porter, and Julius Cook.

Ray's students took his revolution on the road. They have lectured before millions of people over the years across this continent and overseas. Ray's messages of peace, ecological sanity, and world unity have now found a permanent place in various environmental movements, while his lessons in Mohawk history have sparked a rebirth of the longhouse tradition at Akwesasne.

It is no exaggeration to say Ray Fadden's innovative teaching methods and grasp of history have been responsible for a new wave of scholarship in America, one which has finally begun to treat Natives as fully functioning human beings who have contributed greatly to the world.

Ray has retired to his mountain in the Adirondacks north of Saranac Lake along with his wife Christine. He keeps busy feeding the animals and lecturing at the Six Nations Museum he built in the small town of Onchiota. His son, the nationally acclaimed artist John Fadden-Kahionhes, lives nearby to oversee the daily activities of the museum. To this special place Iroquois people will go, as if on a pilgrimage, for spiritual renewal. Ray and Christine assure them of traditional Mohawk hospitality where the hours pass in deep and friendly discussion with this remarkable couple. Their clear and obvious love and respect for each other is an inspiration to all and an example of what true partnership can accomplish.

As fiery as ever, Ray continues to speak out on behalf of historical truth. A genuine visionary, he never wavered from his commitment to improve upon what he was given and to leave an indelible mark across the generations.

TENACIOUS MAISIE SHENANDOAH
Oneida Nation Lives in the Hearts of its Women

Born during the gloomiest days of the Great Depression, Maisie Shenandoah is among the most outgoing and friendliest Native woman one will ever meet.

Her childhood was anything but easy, with the family struggling to provide food for eight girls and two boys, but her mother, Mary Cornelius Winder, was determined not to be defeated by poverty, racism, or anything else.

A descendant of John Skenando, also known as Chief Shenandoah, Mary Winder felt a deep sense of belonging to the hills and valleys of central New York. She was a member of the Wolf Clan Oneida, the matron of a people who lent critical assistance to General George Washington during the American Revolution only to have their homes put to the torch by revenge-minded British allies.

Skenando endured the years of deprivation and hunger to secure the sacred pledges of the infant United States to protect the territorial and political integrity of the Oneida Nation. He lived to see his people dishonored, dismissed, and dispossessed as the federal government refused to intervene when New York State officials adopted a policy of flagrantly cheating the Oneidas of their land.

Within two generations of the Revolution, the majority of the Oneidas were compelled to abandon New York to live as refugees on the western shores of Lake Michigan or on the banks of the Thames River in western Ontario. New York's scheme was to banish all Iroquois to the barren lands of Kansas, but most Natives refused to go.

Mary Winder's dream was to secure an expansive land base to which all Oneidas might return home. Against great odds she began to file land-claim petitions seeking redress in whatever legal or administrative forum she thought might hear her pleas.

Mary Winder journeyed into the spirit world in 1954 without realizing her goal, but the passion behind it, the absolute righteousness of her cause, was passed on to her daughter, Maisie-Yagolehuyani.

For the past four decades, Maisie has pressed for an Oneida homeland, even when others have given up the fight or passed on, exhausted by the battle. She raised her one son and five daughters on Oneida territory, instructing them in Native customs and history, while keeping the memory of her mother in focus by telling vivid stories of Mary Winder's life.

Maisie made presentations in dozens of schools where she spoke about Oneida history, slowly building an awareness as to the great contributions of her Nation to America. She collected stories and legends from other Iroquois people who knew her modest home was a welcome haven for weary travelers and eager students.

The Shenandoah Trading Post Maisie founded has zigged and zagged across the eastern part of North America, marketing Native crafts, collecting and trading works of art, rekindling friendships, and making new ones. Her friendly spirit is known nationwide.

Somehow, Maisie found the time to press for the building of a longhouse on Oneida territory and accept the great task of serving the people as Wolf Clanmother. In this role she is a spiritual counsellor, political leader, cultural teacher, and social arbitrator. As a clanmother, she represents elders, parents, youths, and the unborn since her mandate is to act as cultural custodian, preserving the rights of the generations two hundred years into the future.

A healthy dose of humor has helped Maisie make it through the tough times, of which there have been plenty. But she, like her mother, has an amazing ability to set things right, holding no grudge and offering up a kind word or funny story, heartfelt advice, and a genuine smile. When the winter months bring the cold north winds, sleet, and snow, you might see her waving to a child to come near so she can give them a hat, scarf, and gloves she's saved for them.

When life's cares set in, Maisie's enthusiasm is rekindled by the memory of her mother, whose words are carefully tended and recalled with joy. She knows time will prove her dream right in the end; the Oneidas will rise from the ashes to once again take their rightful place in the world. Her children, and her children's children, will carry Mary Winder's vision of one people, one land across the generations.

Oneida Nation Wolf Clanmother Maisie Shenandoah. Photo © Joanne Shenandoah.

INDEX

MORE GREAT NATIVE AMERICAN TITLES FROM CLEAR LIGHT PUBLISHING

Education is the key to unlock the future; history is the knowledge and resource of the past; the present exists to put intentions into action. We at Clear Light Publishing are honored and proud to be a part of a link to disseminate the wealth of Native American culture through our publications. Below are some of our currently available titles:

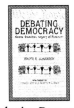

Debating Democracy

Native Science

American Indian History I & II

Ecocide of Native America

One Nation Under God

Children Left Behind

Exiled in the Land of the Free

A People's Ecology

Circle of Life

Po'pay

*Rolling Thunder
Speaks*

*Singing for a
Spirit*

Pueblo Nations

Reuben Snake

*A Time Before
Deception*

Pueblo Profiles

Sacred Fireplace

Utopian Legacies

FOR MORE INFORMATION
WWW.CLEARLIGHTBOOKS.COM
ORDER ON LINE

CLEAR LIGHT PUBLISHING
SANTA FE, NEW MEXICO
1-800-253-2747

*White Roots of
Peace*

Printed in the United States
204442BV00001B/383/A

9 781574 160536